MW01602554

# MAKE MONEY ONLINE
# BLOGGING

A BEGINNERS' 30 DAY STEP BY STEP GUIDE TO
MAKING MONEY BLOGGING ONLINE

## DARREN LAMAR

# MAKE MONEY ONLINE BLOGGING

*A Beginners' **30 Day** Step By Step Guide to Making Money Blogging Online*

*A Device and Internet Are the Only Tools Required To Make Money Blogging Online*

*By: Darren Lamar*

# INTRODUCTION

Let's assume you have a passion or hobby, topics, and ideas you could talk about for years without getting bored or tired.

Rightfully, you decide to do one right thing: start a blog, a platform that allows you to write about your experiences, express your passion, and even go further to educate, encourage, and inspire people.

At first, blogging is a very fulfilling thing to do, and you enjoy every element of the journey. However, down the line, you realize that you wish to make money from your blog; after all, you've heard of tons of people who make lots of money and live lavishly from blogging.

Unfortunately, even though you've heard that tons of bloggers make "good money" from blogging, you can't seem to get things right!

**Here's the truth:**

Yes, blogging is one of the best ways to generate income. Blogging is also one of the simplest ways to make money online. That's because all you need to have is an internet-connected device and tips and tricks that can help turn your blog into an income-generating venture.

There is no unique talent required. All you need to become a successful blogger is hard work, persistence, consistency, and applying the right strategies; a healthy combination of these strategies will keep the money coming in.

- Do you have a blog but are still struggling to monetize it or make a substantial income from it?
- Would you like to start an income-generating blog using the most effective, tried, and tested strategies?

If your answer is a resounding "YES," then you have come to the right place. In this book, we will painstakingly cover everything you need to know about blogs, from:

- How to write great content,
- How to improve visibility on search engines,
- How to market yourself, and more importantly,
- The different ways of making money both actively and passively using your blog,
- *And so much, much more!*

If you're excited to get started, let's jump right into it:

# 1

## UNDERSTANDING BLOGGING BASICS

Let's start from the basics; what is a blog, blogging, blog posts, and blogger?

A blog, sometimes also called a weblog, is an online diary or journal that you can use to can share your opinions, other people's stories, links to other websites, and more. You can write blog posts, post videos or images, and do anything that pleases you and your audience.

Blog posts are the content you create on your blog. The freshest content always appears first on a blog. In other words, a blog registers blog posts in reverse chronological order.

The process of sharing your content is what we call blogging.

A blogger is a person that runs the blog, which, in this case, is you. Because it's pertinent, let's discuss how a blog differs from a regular website:

## What Is The Difference Between A Blog and A Regular Website?

Many people confuse the term "blog" and "website," while many others use the terms interchangeably, which is wrong because although the terms are related, they are slightly different.

The fact is, a blog is a type of website. It differs from a website in terms of how the content gets displayed. A blog will display the freshest content first; we called this "reverse chronological order of posts."

On the other hand, websites tend to be static, with the content arranged or organized on different pages. With websites, it doesn't matter which content was the oldest or newest; the page you place your content is where you will find it.

Websites can also have a blog section if they want and perhaps use it to educate or inform their audience or customers about new happenings, something usually common with business websites.

To conclude, we can say that besides being a unique kind of website used to share information, a blog can also be a part of a website, but a website cannot be part of a blog.

## Why You Need To Start A Blog Today

Let's discuss why you should start a blog today—if you haven't already done so. The good thing is that you don't have to be a professional writer to start blogging; anyone can do it. Besides, blogging will help you know more about content writing and creation, both of which are valuable and marketable business skills in the modern world.

Here are some good reasons why you should start a blog.

# To Make Money

Creating an income-generating blog is this book's focus for a good reason: blogging can make you lots of money.

To make things better, you will be making this money passively, which means money will keep trickling into your bank account even when you're sleeping, at a party, or doing any other fun things you love to do.

Research has shown that successful bloggers spend less than 6 hours per day blogging but make thousands of dollars a month—some successful bloggers spend as little as an hour a day on their blogs. Most people have reported spending 0-6 hours on creating a blog post.

When you start blogging, don't expect to start making thousands of dollars in a month; that's not how it goes. You will get there, but it takes time, and as you shall learn later, the more traffic you attract, the more money you stand to make in the end.

That said, you should note that blogging is a full-time job for the people that get it right. For those that take it as such, blogging is a lucrative occupation. For example, someone like Nick Denton, the founder of Gawker, a blog that focuses on celebrities and the media industry, is worth over $100 million.

Here is a resource with a list of other multi-million dollar bloggers we have today: https://addicted2success.com/news/the-top-10-famous-multi-million-dollar-bloggers/

**It Is Very Affordable To Start**
Blogging is a lucrative business you can start for free. Wordpress.com, Google Blogger, wix.com, Weebly, and more all offer free blogging services.

However, I highly recommend that you start a self-hosted blog for reasons we shall discuss later; fortunately, even self-hosted blogs are affordable.

For example, if you choose to use a blogging platform like wordpress.org, you will need to pay for a hosting service like Bluehost, which charges only $2.95 per month. In a year, that's $35.4, meaning it costs approximately $35 to have your own space on the web.

How affordable is that?

A hosting service allows you to store all your files online—your code, images, videos, letters, etc.—and avails it for people to see.

Free platforms like wix.com, blogger.com, etc., will store these files for you, making it like having your own online space, but through someone else. However, they will control most factors in your blog, like the themes you use, the URL will contain their name, etc.

On the other hand, with self-hosted blogs, you have complete control; you can design your website as you want, use any URL you wish, and more.

**Blogging is Straightforward**
Blogging is easy to start. To get started, you need a computer and an internet connection. The faster the internet, the better; you also need a good laptop and computer—it makes working easier and efficient.

You don't have to be a programmer, have a degree, or some fancy training to create a blog. Most existing blogging platforms are very user-friendly. By that, I mean they provide you with everything you need to set up your blog. You can pick one of the themes they offer and customize it to create something you like that is unique to you.

Additionally, your blog is a personal space where you can do or say anything you want. You will create content on the subjects you find amusing and things you like with no restrictions. You can write in your unique style, the way that you want. If you have ever written an email or conversed with your best friend, you have more than half of what you need to become a successful blogger. The rest is just marketing and learning how to make money through your content, which we will discuss in this guidebook.

However, blogging can be a little demanding too. You need to keep up with your niche and produce quality, relevant content that will keep your audience interested and returning for more. You will have to research your audience to understand them better to ensure you produce content they love.

### A Blog Helps You Improve Your Writing Skills

Starting a blog will have a significant impact on your writing and selling ability. When you begin, blogging will feel a little alien and sometimes awkward; it might even be quite challenging.

However, over time, you will naturally become good at it. It will become a little easier. Words will begin flowing with efficiency, and people will love your style. Your creativity will improve, and you will always find something to write or talk about in your next blog post. You will even learn how to make a great long story from a small thing.

With time, you will also realize the writing style or content that resonates with your audience, which will help you easily and quickly capture their attention, and in the process, enhance your marketing skills.

As you can imagine, if you can capture peoples' attention, you can easily sell them anything you want.

This skill will prove influential later when you want to sell something through your blog.

A blog is a platform for learning as much as it is for making money. After some time, you will become more evolved or wiser than you are today.

### You Will Learn Other Key Skills

You will create a blog to talk about a niche you are passionate about or subjects you like. As you will learn, it is much easier to start a blog that talks about a specific topic, and after that, maybe expand and talk about other things you might want to write about on your blog.

However, for starters, you will choose a niche. For example, you can blog about computer gadgets and their accessories. When starting your blogging journey, you will have basic knowledge about computers and the few gadgets you have come across.

With time, you will need more content or ideas in your niche and will have no choice but to research computers, accessories, and how to use them. You will become an expert in that niche to a point where you will even begin to learn more about how it relates to other niches. In the process, you will learn more about other fields. The knowledge you will gain through blogging will be tremendous.

Besides, you will also learn more about blogs, websites, search engines, email marketing, social media, and more. You will be using these platforms regularly when blogging, and thus, you will need to know them deeper to make the most out of them.

For instance, you will understand how search engines work, from their algorithms to how they rank websites and blogs. The knowledge can make all the difference in your career and life in general.

### Blogging Helps You Confront Your Fears, Insecurities, and Other Issues

A blog is like an online diary. You can talk about yourself, your fears, insecurities, business problems, life, and everything. It puts you out there and allows you to share your thoughts and ideas.

By blogging, you will find and interact with many people who are just like you or who have gone through the challenges you may be facing. It will be very comforting to talk and share with people that understand you, people who you probably wouldn't have met if it wasn't for your blog.

It's a fact that most people use their blog as a platform to confront their fears, overcome their insecurities, and build their confidence and self-esteem.

### Meeting New People
Also, blogging allows you to make new friends, business partners, mentors, clients, customers, etc. It exposes you to the world, allowing you to meet anyone and everyone.

You will find people that share interests similar to yours, like-minded people. For example, if you love cooking and trying out new recipes, you will easily meet other people who love cooking the way you do.

When you start a blog, keep in mind that there are so many people out there that would love to know you, embrace you, and read your content. All you have to do is show up through your blog.

### Land Your Dream Job
If you are a writer, especially a copywriter or a content marketer, you will need a blog that people can look at to gauge if you are worth hiring. Your blog will act as your portfolio and resume.

Your next big employer might come across your blog and love how you talk to people or command a crowd. They will then ask you if you can market for them or join their marketing team to boost sales.

On other occasions, when applying for writing or content creation jobs or landing a client, you can use a blog to show your expertise.

As you can see, starting a blog has a lot of benefits to offer, which is why you should start one today.

Before we dive into how to get started, take a moment to complete this exercise:

### Action step

Why do you want to start a blog? Which of the benefits mentioned above do you connect with the most? Take a journal and write down all the reasons why starting a blog excites you. These reasons will be your core drivers. They'll motivate you to put in the necessary work.

## 2

## HOW TO START A BLOG

Blogging is very rewarding, and starting a blog can easily be one of the best things you will ever do.

For one, it helps you build an online presence that revolves around the things you love and enjoy, sharpens your writing skills, educates you, and, more importantly, you can use it to make money.

Furthermore, you get to educate, motivate and inspire your audience.

Starting a blog can seem daunting if you haven't done it before. You might be wondering,

———

*"How do I get an online presence, a domain, and design a good-looking blog when I don't know anything about programming or building a website?"*

In this chapter, we shall walk through all the steps involved in starting a blog from ideation to publication, along with all the tools you need to make your blogging journey a success.

The process is quite simple to follow, and if you take the various actions we shall discuss in this chapter, you should have your blog up and running in no time.

If you're eager and excited, let's begin

**Choosing The Right Niche**

Before you do anything else, the first thing you need to do is choose a niche, industry, or topic around which your blog shall revolve.

It's not ideal to start a blog that talks about anything and everything because, for one, your blog will be somewhat unsettled. You will be confusing your audience when you talk about cooking tips today, politics tomorrow, tech the day after tomorrow, and parenting problems the day after that.

Choosing a niche will also help you decide which domain name to use for your blog. Besides, when you work with a specific niche, it is much easier to market your blog and monetize it through affiliate links.

As you can see, choosing a niche is one of the most important things you will have to do when creating a blog because this is where your blog will revolve around. Thus this step is one you must carefully consider and think through before concluding.

Before discussing how to choose a blogging niche, let's first discuss some basics things about a blogging niche:

## What Is A Blogging Niche?

A niche is the main topic or theme of your blog. For example, if you decide to start a blog about sports, your niche will be sports. You can even specialize further to talk about a specific kind of sport; for example, you can create a blog that talks only about weightlifting and bodybuilding sports. In this instance, we will say that your niche is "weightlifting and bodybuilding."

## Why Is It Important To Choose A Niche?

Here are some reasons why choosing a niche is very important.

### It gives you authority over your industry
If you want an answer or information about a specific question, say SEO, will you trust a blog that talks about SEO specifically or a general blog featuring only one or two posts about SEO?

Like most people, you will go for the blog specifically created to talk about the topic you are interested in—SEO in this case. That is the power of selecting a niche: it makes people and search engines believe that you are the expert in that particular field.

As we shall discuss later when discussing search engine optimization, you will see how this "authority" is a key factor that search engines consider when deciding where to rank websites on their index.

### It is much easier to attract loyal readers when you have a niche

When people know [exactly] what to expect from you, it will be much easier for them to come back to your blog. This phenomenon is akin to going to a steak restaurant that has a unique steak recipe you like. You will always go back to that restaurant to order that steak.

Another example is a bar that plays good jazz music. If you like jazz, you will always go to that bar to listen to jazz, even when other bars play the same music genre. The same applies to blogs.

If someone finds that your blog provides good information about a particular topic, they will always look for you whenever they want information related t that topic or niche. These audiences will become your loyal, repeat audience. It is essential to have such kinds of readers because they will become your free brand ambassadors.

### It will become much easier to make money

If you want to make money easily and quickly with your blog, try niche blogging. When you have a loyal, targeted audience, it will be much easier to sell targeted items.

For example, if your blog is about weightlifting and body-building, your targeted audience will be gym-goers. Thus, it will be much easier to sell these people gym equipment and supplements.

Since they are already interested in matters gym, it won't

take much convincing to convince them to purchase your recommendations. That's how important niche blogging is to blog monetization.

You get a targeted audience truly interested in that field, who won't think much before making a purchase when you sell them something in that field.

As you can see, you should pick your niche today. However, while picking your niche, there are some factors you need to consider.

## Factors To Consider When Choosing A Niche

Here are some important factors to consider when choosing a blogging niche:

### The purpose of your blog
What do you aim to achieve with your blog?

Besides making money, do you also want to educate and inspire, or is your core aim to have fun and connect with people online?

If you are blogging as a hobby, you can do it for the pleasure it gives without minding about money. You don't need to stress about finding a niche. Instead, have a more relaxed approach and choose something that will keep you going because you enjoy it too much.
On the other hand, if you want to blog to make make money, which is at the heart of this guidebook, your approach to choosing a niche requires a degree of consideration.

You will need to pick a niche you know is profitable, something with a degree of competition you can handle. If the niche you are interested in is very flooded, for example, the parenting niche, you can choose to be more specific. For example, you can focus on single mother parenting tips or challenges, single dad parenting tips, being a parent to a child with disabilities, etc.

Generally speaking, pick a niche that aligns with your purpose.

### Are you passionate about it?

You must be passionate about the niche you choose; otherwise, you will get bored quickly.

Passion for your niche will keep you going even before you start making the amount of money you want. Besides, your readers will easily tell if you are enthusiastic about what you are talking about or not.
Here's the rule when it comes to this:

If you can't write naturally about a particular topic, leave it alone because you can't be passionate about something you don't know or want to know more about on a blog.

What you want to talk about must have inspired you so much that you took your free time to learn about it and still feel excited to learn more about it as you share with your audience.

Another factor that closely relates to passion is your expertise or your profession. For instance, if you are good at cooking, loved it to the point where you went to study it, and ended up becoming a chef, it will be more appropriate for you to start a cooking blog because this is something you know, love, and have been doing for years. The same goes for your current job. If you love your job, you can start a blog about related career issues and how to be better at it.

Lastly, you should make sure that you have a lot to talk about regarding your passion or expertise—an endless supply of ideas.

This prospect should not worry you all that much because, down the line, you will find something to talk about with continued research and blog review. Blogging gets to a point where your readers will give you ideas on what to talk about next, which happens through engagement.

We shall discuss this more in the next chapter as we discuss how to grow your blog and notice it.

### Can you make money from your chosen niche?

Blogging for money comes down to profits. Is your niche profitable?

If you can't see a way to make money in your chosen niche, or if you have limited making money opportunities, then even when you are passionate about the topic, it will be a wasted effort.

The only exception to this is when you're blogging for pleasure, which defeats this book's purpose: making money through blogging.

Knowing if your niche is profitable will require you to do some research. You should scout other bloggers in your industry to see if they have also made money using their blogs. If they are making money, then you will do. Don't worry too much about the competition. If the market is healthy enough, you all stand to make money in the long run.

The alltop.com tool will help you find popular blogs in your niche. Study those blogs to see how they are making money. For instance, you will easily notice banner ads, affiliate links, sponsored posts, etc.

### Can you also sell personally-created products?

Another key factor to consider when choosing your niche is whether it's possible to sell personal products on your blog, especially if you have a business or intend to start a business in the future.

For example, Neil Patel, founder of neilpatel.com, blogs about things to do with online marketing, from website SEO tips, content marketing tips, search engine marketing, email, and social media marketing, and more.

He founded an online service called Kissmetrics that you can use to analyze how your website, blog, social media account, and other online tools you use in marketing are performing. He sells this service on his blog/website.

You can see that his niche closely relates to the product he sells to his audience.

Okay, now you know the factors you need to consider to ensure that you choose the right niche. How should you go about it?

**Action step**

To choose a niche, do the following :

Start with a brainstorming session. Brainstorming is a great way to generate ideas or know yourself and your purpose better through lateral thinking.

The process entails sitting in a quiet, peaceful place, generating ideas without criticism or worrying about what is too crazy or out of the box. In other words, we can say that brainstorming is a free form of creative thinking.

A good brainstorming session should help you visualize what you want for yourself or give you more ideas on what you want to do.

If you are going to brainstorm, there are some rules you must adhere to; they include:

Generate as many ideas as you can; don't limit yourself. There's no such thing as too much. Don't consider any idea "crazy." All ideas are worth exploring and understanding.

If you have existing ideas, you should expound them or break them down into other chunks of ideas. If you are brainstorming with another person, never criticize the person's ideas. With that in mind, here are some brainstorming basics to get you started.

Start by thinking about why you want the blog in the first place. What do you aim to accomplish? What's your purpose?

Think about what interests you. Go for something you will still enjoy doing or discussing four years from now and 100 articles later. Think about what you have a solid knowledge or expertise on. Sometimes, we say, "Something you can do easily, even without thinking about and without the prospect of making money from it." That could be your profession, side hustle, or a hobby that you are good at, or anything else.

Think about your experiences. What are some of the big lessons you have learned from life? What are some of the life events you experienced that stuck with you? What about your daily life ventures can you share with other people?

Move further to the things you love to read or watch. Why do you love reading the books, blogs, articles, and magazines you normally look for, read, watch, etc.? What's in them that captures your interest? Do the same to the movies you watch.

You can also think about your environment. Why do you love where you live, the places you have visited, your furniture, and more? Gather as many reasons as possible to ensure that you have a clear understanding of what you love and can do for a long time.

You will need a pen and paper during this session. For instance, if you are thinking about everything you enjoy, write down as many ideas as you can. Afterward, find the ideas that relate to each other and join them. Then take that single idea as your main topic of the brainstorming session. From here, you can find so many different things you can talk about in your blog.

Besides the questions, you can also use a brainstorming technique called a SWOT Analysis.

A SWOT analysis involves determining your **S**trengths, **W**eaknesses, **O**pportunities, and **T**hreats.

To use this approach, create a quadrant and label each box

with what you want to determine. Have something like this in the end -

S trengths

Weaknesses

Opportunities

Threats

You use this information to identify a niche that will make sure that you can capitalize on your strengths, build on your weaknesses, minimize or understand the things you find threatening, and help you get and embrace as many opportunities as you can. An opportunity can be a way of making profits.

After finding your purpose and passion through that brainstorming session, it is time to think about the money.

Does your niche have numerous money-making opportunities? Are there affiliate schemes within your niche? Can you sell your products? Can third-party ad services like AdSense work with you? Consider these and other such questions.

Profits work based on demand and supply. For instance, is there enough demand for the product or services within your niche? If yes, you can use your blog as a platform that will help your audience and other people get what they want.

You can also create demand by promoting a product. For example, if you sell your products, you can convince people by focusing on bringing out why they should buy your product. In a nutshell, here is a quick summary of the action steps you should take to find a profitable blogging niche:

**Step 1:** Use the brainstorming session to find a minimum of 3-5 different niches you can blog about comfortably and from which you can make money.

**Step 2:** Thoroughly analyze each of your chosen niches and determine which in which niche you can make the most money. You can determine this by looking at the number of people that interact with that particular niche, the competition, and of course, the amount of money you can make from that niche.

It is easy to feel threatened by stiff competition within a niche; don't let competition scare you. Remember that there is competition everywhere. You will always get some traffic at the end of the day. Just focus on how you can stand out from the rest. Besides, competition is the best way to determine the making money potential within a niche.

To help you get started on choosing a niche, here are some profitable niches. You can go with these or niche down to any related area within these niches.

- Finance
- Making money online
- Technology

- Dating and relationships
- Health
- Fitness
- Beauty and fashion
- Self-Help
- Do It Yourself and Home Decor
- Travel

As mentioned, you can specify further in these niches. Let's use tech as an example. Tech is extremely broad; therefore, you should find a specific, tech-related area to focus on.

After choosing a niche, your next focus should be choosing an ideal blogging platform:

**Choose A Blogging Platform (Advantages, Disadvantages, and Price Point)**

A blogging platform is an online service or software that allows you to create, publish, and manage your content on the internet.

It makes it possible for anyone with an internet connection can access your blog, read, share, or comment on your blog posts. In other words, a blogging platform stores your content, files, media, links, and other things necessary to keep your blog working at its best. Think of it as an online library that stores your books.

If anyone wants to read something you wrote, they will find it in the library. Afterward, they can comment, discuss with you, or even recommend that book to their friends. A blogging platform is your online library.

A simple Google search will reveal many blogging platforms from which to choose. Before you jump on any of them, here are some of the factors you should consider before picking any platform.

## Factors To Consider When Choosing A Blogging Platform

Here are the important factors to consider when choosing a blogging platform—you can consider these your action plans for this step:

### User-friendliness

You'd do well to choose a user-friendly blogging platform. It should be something that will make setting up and operating your blog easy while giving your audience a great experience when on your blog.

If you are a newbie, you will need something easy to use. By that, I mean you should go for a blogging platform that is easy to navigate, manage, add content, edit, update, and more, without having coding or other special computer skills. It should also be easy to install and set up a blog without any difficulties.

Besides, your audience should also have an easy time navigating your blog. People have a short attention plan and limited patience. If your blog isn't user-friendly, you will disenfranchise many people who could have been your loyal audience.

## Customization

Although it's important to go with a blogging platform that frontloads most of the work—a blog that is self-explanatory to use—it will reach a point—mostly 2 to 3 years later—where you will feel like you need some new functionalities and design.

For instance, you will feel like you need a unique layout specific to your blog, graphics, and more. Thus, it's ideal to choose a blogging platform that allows you to customize your blog without any hassle.

Free blogging platforms allow you to choose a range of pre-designed themes; others give you the ability to add functions like RSS, a web feed that allows you to access updates on your different blogposts. For example, if new content gets published on your blog, details about that content will be provided to you, including the link, summary, full text, etc.

These features are good, but if you want to take it a notch higher, say with specialized customization, switch servers, have complete control, and no third-party involvement, opt for paid blogging platforms. Go for something robust that will make it easier to grow as your blog or business grows.

Many bloggers start with a free platform, build a good reputation, and when their blog grows, they move on to a new self-hosted platform. Here's the thing: It's painful to leave something you have built for a long time to move onto a more robust platform that satisfies your needs.

My advice is to start with a platform you will continue to use ten years from now. The good thing is that most of these platforms are affordable. For instance, wordpress.org, one of the best blogging platforms, uses Bluehost hosting and only costs $35.4 a year.

## Safety and security

As much as blogging is fun, you will also need your blog to make money. Therefore, it is crucial to ensure that your chosen blogging platform is safe and secure for all the money transactions you want.

Free-hosted platforms are under the governance of third-party agencies that have various policies and procedures.

It might reach a point where the third-party agencies may want to change or update their policies and procedures, which may affect your business or income streams for some time. It might even cause complications to your users; for example, they will wonder why transaction terms or procedures have changed.

Besides, because it's online, a blog can get malicious attacks from hackers. You should make sure that the platform you choose a robust system that prevents attacks on your blog.

However, be keen. Most of these attacks happen when you are accessing your blog using a public network. Therefore, to avoid such attacks, the first thing you should do is avoid public networks. Use your WI-FI at home or use mobile data when out in public.

## Monetization opportunities

Monetization opportunities are the different ways you will use to earn revenues from your blog. Choose a blogging platform that allows you to monetize in as many different ways as you wish. Some blog platforms may restrict some blog monetization approaches—besides selling personal products.

Therefore, conduct thorough research on the platform you plan to use to see if it will allow you to use various ways to monetize your blog. It can be disheartening and painful to invest your time, energy, and resources into creating a world-class blog only to get limited by your chosen blogging platform.

**Search engine friendliness**
For your blog to be visible and easily findable by internet users, search engine platforms should rank you high on the search engine results page.

For example, if your blog is about cooking and you have covered recipes for preparing lasagna, if I type "how to cook lasagna," your blog should appear under my search results. When that happens, it will be much easier to click on your link and visit your blog. That's what search engine friendliness can do for you.

Thus, when choosing a blogging platform, go one preferred by almost all the major search engines, including but not limited to Google, Yahoo, DuckDuckGo, Bing, Baidu, Ask.-com, and Yandex.
If your blog is search engine friendly, it will be much easier to reach a wider audience, and you will garner a huge following much quicker and easier. A bigger following will lead to easy conversions and thus more revenues. We shall also look at how to optimize your blog for search engines later in this guide.

## Budget

Your budget is another key consideration to have in mind when choosing a blogging platform. Of course, free platforms seem enticing because they are, well, free. However, although they serve the basic functions of a blog, they are often limited, and you don't have full control over your blog.

I would recommend putting up a small investment for your blog. If I'm truthful, if you are serious about making good money from blogging, invest in high-quality self-hosted platforms.

Different self-hosted platforms have different prices. Based on what you want to achieve with your blog, you will choose one over the others. Let's look at the different platforms and their budgets next.

## The Main Blogging Platforms

Here are the commonly used blogging platforms that you should consider:

- Wordpress.org
- Wordpress.com
- Wix.com
- Medium.com
- Blogger.com
- Tumblr
- Ghost
- Weebly
- Squarespace

Let's talk about the merits and demerits of each, including who each platform is ideal for:

**1: WordPress.org**

**NOTE:** Don't confuse this with WordPress.com, which is the free alternative of wordpress.org.

Wordpress.org is the most popular blogging platform used today. Popular websites and blogs like Vogue India, Flickr, Star Wars News, Variety magazine, and rapper Snoop Dogg use WordPress.org as their blogging platform.

This blogging platform is open-source, which means it has a huge active community of users that constantly develop and update its plugins, widgets, and other functionalities to make it function at its best.
The platform provides an easy-to-use blog, even for beginners, and you can further customize it to match your design and functionality preference. The platform also provides a wide range of monetization opportunities. You can monetize however you want, which is different from wordpress.com.

To use this platform, you will need a web hosting provider. A web host is a company that rents out web server technologies and services that help host your website on the internet.

In other words, for a fee, your host provider will allow you to rent the server on which you will host your website or blog. This server is important because it ensures that when someone types your URL into a browser, their phones or computer will connect to the server you have rented. Wordpress.org commonly uses Bluehost for its hosting.

Now:

**Wordpress.org are ideal for you if:**

- You're looking to make money with your blog without any monetization limitations.
- You wish to integrate your blog into your business website in the future or now. As we discussed earlier, some platforms like wordpress.org enable you to add a blogging section to your business website.
- You are a professional writer or blogger—or hoping to become one with time. The reality is that people tend to take self-hosted blogs more seriously because it shows professionalism.
- You want more control over your blog. If you want to customize your blog however you want, install plugins, control ads, and any other thing on your platform, this platform is for you.

**Advantages of wordpress.org**

- You have complete control over monetization and customization.
- There are incredible amounts of plugins you can add to your blog to make it much better or ensure it functions [exactly] how you want it to function.
- It is much easier to add other extra features on wordpress.org like email subscription sign-up forms, eCommerce, and other forum features.
- Wordpress.org has a vast number of free and premium themes you can choose. The wordpress.org community keeps working to produce the most professional and slick-looking themes you can use

for your blog. You don't even need a web designer to have the best-looking website on the internet.

- Last but not least, wordpress.org is reputable for being search engine friendly. Search engines love this platform, and thus, using it improves your chances of ranking higher on the Search engine results page (SERPs).

**Disadvantages of wordpress.org**

- It isn't free; this platform requires you to self-host your blog, which means you will need to prepare a budget. Luckily, wordpress.org is very affordable.
- You will have to be vigilant to ensure that you know when they release an update, which you will then have to install. Fortunately, this process is usually easy, and in most instances, WordPress auto-updates.
- You will also have to keep your plugins updated. That means you will have to check with the company you obtained your plugins from to check if they have produced an update.

**How much you need to start using wordpress.org**

It is free to signup, download, and use wordpress.org. However, you will need to rent web hosting services. The commonly wordpress.org web host is

Bluehost.com, which only costs $2.95 a month for a 36 months plan. You will also need to get a free domain name that costs $15. A domain name is your blog's address, your URL.

In total, you will need $106.2 to host your site for 3 years for the 36-month plan rate. To that, add the $15 for the domain name, bringing your total to $121.2, which is pretty much affordable.

## 2: Wordpress.com

If you want a free and simple blogging platform from Word-Press, then wordpress.com is for you. With this option, you don't need to worry about self-hosting your blog. Wordpress.com provides you free hosting service, a custom domain name—however, wordpress.com will appear along-side your URL, for example, yoursite.wordpress.com—the ability to share on social media, blog polls, and comments functionality.

Wordpress.com is 100% free. However, if you want to pay for some premium upgrades, you can do so. Besides, the support and the wordpress.com community are always active and willing to answer any questions you may have about your wordpress.com blog.
The platform has numerous tutorials you can view and learn from, including how to get started, customize, and drive traffic to your blog. And thus, all the information you may want to make your blog the best one yet is available for you for free.

Unlike wordpress.org, wordpress.com doesn't allow you to monetize your blog. You won't run Google AdSense and other affiliate marketing networks on your blog.

## Wordpress.com is ideal for:

- A hobby blogger.
- Anyone who wants a simple blog without any costs or a long installation process.
- If you want to write for people without monetizing your blog.
- If you are new to blogging and want to test your blogging skills.

## Advantages of wordpress.com

- It is easy to use.
- Simple to set up.
- It is 100% free

## Disadvantages

- It doesn't allow you to monetize your blog. Therefore, if you are into making money with your blog, this platform isn't for you.
- It has severely limited customization abilities. The platform provides you with pre-designed themes that you select to use.
- There will be a WordPress logo on your blog.
- Your domain name will contain wordpress.com.
- It doesn't have an HTML editor. HTML editors allow you to add other custom features that you may want on your blog.
- WordPress will run its ads on your site. It's giving you everything for free, so they will use your platform to run their ads to compensate themselves for giving you valuable server space.
- There're limitations to the number of plugins you

can, and you cannot install external plugins.
- Limited server storage—a maximum of 3GB.
- If WordPress feels like you are violating their terms and conditions, they will shut down your blog with very little notice. You are not the one in control.

How much it costs to start using wordpress.com
Wordpress.com is free, but you can also upgrade to the premium version.

The premium version ensures no WordPress logo, no WordPress ads, and you get a custom domain name, i.e., instead of www.yoursite.wordpress.com, it will be www.yoursite.com.

The above upgrades will cost you $2.99 per month.

**3: Wix.com**

Wix.com is another famously used blogging platform. It hosts over 160 million websites, and many big websites like the Black Hound Design Company, NoraMinno, a certified personal trainer and dietitian in New York, and many others use wix.com.

This platform features a drag-and-drop feature that allows users to build their blogs or websites fast and easily. Besides, there are hundreds of free templates you can choose from and use for your blog.

Wix.com has a web-based interface but comes highly optimized for mobile phones and tablets.
It is a self-hosted platform, meaning you need a customized

domain name, have total control over your blog, and can customize your blog however you see fit.

### Advantages of wix.com

- The platform has remarkable templates with exceptional designs. The layouts are available for almost all industries.
- Wix has a straightforward setup process. It even offers an artificial intelligence smart assistant you can use when creating your website. The smart assistant will automatically connect to your social media pages to see which template design is the most appropriate for your audience—you can change the template and even turn off the assistant if you don't want to use it.
- Wix offers an easy-to-use interface both for you and your audience.
- Wix also allows for monetization opportunities.
- It comes out-of-the-box highly optimized for mobile devices, which is a plus.

### Disadvantages

- Compared to wordpress.org, Wix customization options are a bit lacking. Wix's initial design purpose was for websites, but it also provides a platform for blogging.
- The free Wix version has lots of ads that will interrupt your audience all the time when they are reading your blog. If you must use Wix, pay for the premium version.
- You cannot change your theme once you select it when building your blog. If you feel like you have to

change the theme, you will have to rebuild your blogsite afresh.
- Wix has slow loading speeds, which gives them a disadvantage in SEO ranking. Although Wix sites perform well when it comes to ranking, they're not as good as wordpress.org.

### How much it cost to use Wix.com

Wix has a free version that contains ads and subdomain URLs. Avoid this when you are serious about making money with your blog.

You pay $5/month to use a personalized domain name. However, Wix will still show their ads on your site. If you pay $14/month, you get to use a personal domain name, no ads, and you get plenty of storage.

If you need extra site space of up to 10GB, you will need an $18/month plan.

There's also a VIP plan that costs $23 per month. This plan allows you to create an online store for your business and use Wix premium apps like Wix bookings.

### Wix is ideal for you if:

- You want to monetize your blog.
- You intend to start an online business in the future.
- If you are—or intend to become—a professional writer and blogger.
- Beginners; the free version is ideal for beginners who are looking to test the waters of blogging.

## 4: Blogger.com

Blogger.com was the pioneer of all the blogging platforms. It started as early as 1999 when people still didn't know much about blogging. Google owns it, and thus, you can expect it to perform wonderfully in Google rankings, which it does.

Blogger.com is a free blogging platform that is very easy to set up and use. It allows you to monetize and edit HTML, which is very hard to find on free blogging platforms. You can add widgets, embedded videos, images, photos, gifs and publish content for your audience to see. It offers a variety of themes you can choose from and even change.

Blogger.com is the best free blogging platform you will find on the internet today.

### Blogger.com is ideal for you if:

- You are a newbie blogger.
- You're a hobby blogger.
- You're looking to make money with your blog. However, this takes time and a lot of effort. To qualify for AdSense, Google will require you to buy a custom domain name, produce at least 15 well-written posts, and your blog must look clean and professional. Google will also check to see if you have used copyright images. If you have, delete them first before you apply for AdSense.

### How much it costs to use Blogger:
Blogger is 100% free, but you can set up a custom domain name, which typically costs $10 to $15 per year.

### Advantages of blogger.com

- It is easy to use. Even when you haven't used any website or blogging platform before, you will quickly set up and navigate through blogger.
- It is an entirely free platform, with so many great features not found on other free blogging platforms.
- Blogger.com is a very safe and secure platform. Because they have been around since the beginning of blogging, they know how to keep you safe from hackers.
- It ranks well on search engines. This product is from the world's largest search engine, Google, which means it's extremely user and search-engine friendly.

### Disadvantages of blogger

- You won't have complete control over your site. If Google feels like you are not adhering to its terms and conditions, it will shut your site down.
- Customization is limited, and there are no upgrade options. You can only choose one of the pre-designed tools made available for you. After choosing a theme, you will have limited change options. The only thing you will probably change is the theme color.
- When you feel like you have outgrown blogger, it will be very difficult to move your site to other more advanced platforms. Therefore, you will have not choice but to start all over again. You will lose all your traffic and subscribers.
- Blogger has limited storage space, documentation, and support. Blogger provides 1 GB of free storage space. If you want more, you will have to connect it

to your Google Drive or Google plus account, which will offer you an extra 15 GB.

## 5: Medium.com

Medium is one of the latest blogging platforms. It started in 2012 for writers and bloggers focused on producing content. It defines itself as a community of writers and readers, people connected by the intention of sharing and learning. Content strategist Erik Devaney had this to say about this platform:

> *"Medium is not about who you are or whom you know, but about what you have to say."*

———

This platform has a built-in audience visiting with one core purpose: to read your content. Thus, it's ideal for committed writers and bloggers highly invested in expressing solid views and stories about different subjects.

Using Medium is comparable to writing for a magazine. You get a space and an audience; all you have to do is write something that many people will find interesting.

The creators host the platform. That means you cannot use a custom domain, you cannot run your blog on a personal server, and you cannot download anything from the platform.

Medium is akin to a social media site where you log into your profile, publish what you intend to publish, and then post it for people to find. When someone queries something you have discussed on the Medium search engine, your blog will get ranked, not the entire platform. One advantage of the medium.com platform is that it is very search engine friendly.

The platform offers a paid membership program, where they pay you for the number of times people read or interact with your content.

Medium also has an app that allows people to "randomly explore" to find and read your blogs. Medium places your articles in front of the audience. They have a feature where users can choose the specific niches they would love to explore and read. They will then select the blogs in those niches and show them. Your job will be to produce some-thing that most people will like and click on to read.

Medium seeks to give everyone a voice. Meaning it doesn't matter if you have backlinks, thousands of followers, or friends; if you have something interesting and useful to say, Medium will give you a platform on which to do so.

Furthermore, their algorithm prioritizes quality above everything else. Thus, even if your content is three years old but is the best on a topic, Medium will still rank it first on the platform for related keywords. It disobeys the blogging norm of reverse chronological order, where the newest/freshest content appears first.

Medium is one of the simplest platforms to sign up and use. You can sign up within a minute using your email, Facebook, or Google account. You only need to use one, and Medium will automatically use the credentials from either of these accounts to sign you up within a minute.

Medium is a 100% free platform with no premium upgrading options or other extras that you need to purchase to run your blog. The best part is it has over 200 million users who are ready to read your content.

Now:

Medium previously used a "clapping" system to determine how to pay creators, but that feature became defunct in 2019. Today, the platform uses clapping stats as a ranking metric. Clapping is how your readers show that they have appreciated your work—it is similar to liking a post on social media. Therefore, the more claps you get, the higher your chances of ranking higher for related keywords and topics.

Since 2019, Medium has been using 'reading time' to compensate creators. Reading time is the amount of time a user spends reading your post. They found that if people spend more time on your blog or story, it shows that you produce high-quality content, and you deserve compensation for that.

Medium calculates this reading time from paying members, users that have subscribed to Medium. But, non-members will also count if they sign up for Medium within 30 days of reading your story—the platform has a 30-day browser cookie.

The primary disadvantage to Medium is that they don't accept banner ads and other third-party ad programs. They aim to provide their users with the best, easy reading experience, which doesn't include ads. However, they accept affiliate links. If you have a business and want to sell your products, you can add links that lead users back to your business website.

### Advantages of using Medium.com

- The platform is well designed and looks great.
- The platform is easy to use. You don't have to be an expert at coding or blogging to start or run your blog.
- There is a ready-made audience. This eliminates the hassle of finding an audience, allowing you to focus on content creation.
- The platform is 100% free.
- Search engine friendly. Medium will always rank highly on search engines, especially Google, because it has a reputation for high-quality content.

### Disadvantages of using Medium.com

- You lack complete control over your blog. You can't build a platform with a particular design or look. You take what Medium has provided for you and use it. Your content is the only thing that will make you stand out.
- Limited methods of monetizing.
- Medium owns almost everything about your blog. They provide the audience and control the content that you publish

### Medium is ideal for you if:

- You are a professional writer and blogger interested

in publishing quality content for a ready-made audience and looking to build your brand.

- You are a beginner. As we have discussed earlier, Medium is free, simple to set up and use, and it has an audience that is ready and motivated to read what you want to write.
- You are a hobby blogger interested in sharing your views with the world.
- You are someone looking to get paid for blogging. Among all the other platforms, Medium is the only one that pays you for writing. You get appreciated for putting in work and thought into your work.

### How much it costs to use Medium

It is 100% free.

### 6: Tumblr.com

Tumblr is a platform for people interested in visual blogging, and if you love sharing videos, photos, gifs, chats, quotes, music, texts, and links, this is the platform for you. Tumblr's use is common among teens and young adults, and it is more preferred by females than males.

It offers easy sharing and reblogging options, making it easy for your content to reach a much wider audience, especially if you aim to sell your products through your blog.

Automattic Inc owns the Tumblr platform. Therefore, your content must adhere to their terms and regulations. If they feel like what you post is out of line, they will kick you out. However, they freely host your blog and also provide a ready-made audience for your content.

I wouldn't recommend it for a writer.

## The advantages of using Tumblr

- It is free.
- It is easy to integrate with your social media platforms.
- It is easy to set up and use.
- It is much easier to promote your content through this platform. The site has a reblog option button. Therefore, when your audience clicks on it, your content automatically gets republished on their feed.
- They provide various monetization opportunities, such as third-party ad companies like Google AdSense, Bing Ads, Yahoo Ads, Infolinks, etc. You can also use Affiliate links and advertise your products.

## The disadvantages of using Tumblr

- You cannot customize the blog to suit your style. Tumblr provides pre-designed themes with no additional features.
- You cannot export your content when you feel like you have outgrown Tumblr and need a self-hosted platform.

## Tumblr is ideal:

- If you love visual blogging, then Tumblr is perfect for you.
- If you are a microblogger, i.e., if you love publishing small amounts of content along with images or gifs, Tumblr is your best choice.

- If you are new to blogging and still testing the waters, this is the best blogging platform for you. Besides, since the platform is ready and set up for you, you don't need any coding or computer skills to run your blog. Setting up your blog entails entering your email address, password, the username you would like to use, and your age.
- If your audience base is mainly teens and young adults, you can use Tumblr to reach them.
- It is also a good platform for monetizing your blog. It allows affiliate links, ad companies, and you can also sell your products on your page.

**How much it will cost to set up a Tumblr blog:**

Zero; the platform is free.

**7: Weebly.com**

Weebly is one of the best and easy-to-use blogging platforms. This platform hosts over 40 million websites and blogs. It is a great platform to work with and also monetize.

Weebly will fully host your blog on their servers, which means you can operate and manage your site online or through Weebly's App. The storage space is unlimited, but they regulate the size you can allow for a single file. For example, if you are using the free version, the maximum size for a single file you put on your blog will be 100MB. Paid plans allow for a maximum file size from 250MB to 1GB.

The platform has a drag-and-drop feature that allows you to

drag a widget and drop it at different places on your site. Weebly also has high-quality templates with over 60 different designs that will make your blog look bold and beautiful.

Weebly has a free and paid version paid plan. The free version works great and has no time limit. If you are comfortable with the free plan, you can use it for as long as you want. However, the free plan has limited features, no custom domain—meaning your URL will contain '.weebly.com'—and Weebly will show their ads on your page.

If you want to use your domain name, remove all ads, get better features, themes, and other advanced features, you should choose the paid plan. With prices starting at $6 to $26 per month, the paid plan is very affordable.

When it comes to customization, Weebly can only allow you to customize the themes and add other add-ons. You can change things like color, size of elements like the header, footer and content, font style, and other basic elements. The drag-and-drop feature also allows you to edit your source HTML and CSS if you want more features beyond what the Weebly platform offers.

Weebly allows various monetization opportunities, such as affiliate links, ad companies like Google AdSense, Bing ads, etc., and you can also sell your products on a Weebly-based blog.

**Weebly is ideal for:**

- Newbie bloggers with no previous coding and programming skills.

- People with coding and programming skills.
- Anyone interested in making money from a blog.
- Professional bloggers and writers.
- Hobby bloggers.

### Advantages of Weebly.com

- It has a drag-and-drop feature that makes it very easy to customize your blog.
- It has a free version and a premium package. You can go with whichever you are comfortable with at any time. Also, the premium package has different levels. There are different subscription plans for different blogging goals.
- It is simple to set up and manage.
- It is search engine friendly.

### Disadvantages of Weebly

- The free version has limited features.
- If you are not good at coding, you are limited to the themes that Weebly offers.

### How much will it cost

- The free version costs zero.
- The premium version ranges from $6 to $24 a month, depending on the extra features you want from your website.

## 8: Ghost.org

Ghost is another wonderful blogging platform you can use. What makes it special is that its design is specific to blogging, and you get to own everything. You own your content, audience, platform, and the code used to build that platform. That means you can do anything and everything you want with your blog. You can build any categories, format, and flow that agree with your specific needs.

You can customize your URL structures, homepage, and your multi-language content. If you like, you can go as far as adding a logo, navigation menus, including analytics codes, and anything you want. Once you create your account, you can do whatever you like.

The best part is that this platform has a well-optimized design that performs very well on search engines. It has tools like canonical tags, XML sitemaps, permalinks, schematic markup, and automatic Metadata with manual overrides.

These tools help the search engine return more informative results for users. Thus, when people search for anything related to your content, your chances of appearing on the first page are very high. This is one of Ghost's advantages over all the other platforms—including wordpress.org, where you need to install SEO plugins. With Ghosts, the platform comes already optimized for SEO.

Ghost is simple to set and use. It has elegant templates, themes, and everything you need to get started. If you know a bit of coding and would like to have a custom structure, you can do so.

Other great features of Ghost include:

- It uses Unsplash.com images. The platform can loop into Unsplash.com, a site with over a million free and unlicensed images, to show you images that you may use on your content. This feature makes it easy to produce beautiful and attractive content. As you may know, people love blog content with images because it captures their attention.
- It also has a feature known as Newsletter Capture. This feature makes it easy to capture the emails of those that visit your site, making it easier to build an email list of a loyal audience and people you can update every time you produce new content. Besides, you can use this as an opportunity to market or sell your products to them.
- Another important feature is the AMP support. Besides other SEO tools, you can use the AMP tool to improve your search rankings. Ghost provides this out-of-the-box; with other platforms, you will have to install these tools.
- On top of it all, it has a dark mode feature that makes it easy for you to write in the dark without harming your eyes.
- Ghost is a great platform for a blogger. It is one of the few best ones you will find today.

### Advantages of Ghost.org

- Highly optimized for SEO.
- It has various elegant themes that will make your blog stand out in the crowd.
- It directly links to Unsplash.com, making it easy for

you to use free and unlicensed images for your content.

- You can easily connect it to WordPress. If you have a WordPress website for business, you can use the Ghost plugin to directly import or export files between the two platforms.
- It is a lightweight platform made specifically for blogging purposes. Therefore, the loading times are extremely fast, thus preferred by most search engines.
- Ghost uses modern technologies called Node.js, and thus, everything about it is an upgrade of other platforms.
- It has a membership management feature on the dashboard, meaning you can manage users that visit your blogsite.
- It was built exclusively for blogging purposes.
- It uses a markup language known as 'markdown' that splits the screen into two. Thus, when editing your blog, you get an immediate reference of how the final product will look. That makes editing your blog very easy, and you can also learn more about commands when working with Ghost.
- Ghost allows many monetization opportunities, including Google AdSense, Bing Ads, etc.

### Disadvantages of Ghost.org

- Beginners or people that don't know much about coding are only limited to the free and paid templates and themes.
- Self-hosting will require some technical knowledge. If you have no such skills, you can let Ghost.org host for you.

- It has no native comment functionality. Instead, it has an option to implement the comment system that you would like to use. That means you will have to depend on third parties services like Isso to get comments from your audience.

**Ghost is ideal for:**

- Professional bloggers and writers.
- Anyone looking to have complete control over their blogs.
- Ghost has a large marketplace for both free and paid templates. So even a beginner can use this platform.
- Anyone looking to make money online from blogging; since you have full control, you can monetize a Ghost-driven blog whichever way you want.

**How much it costs to use Ghost**

- The open-source Ghost is free, but it requires hosting, which will cost you $10 to $20 per month.
- Ghost pro with a hosting program costs $28 per month.

**9: Squarespace.com**

Just like Weebly and Wix, Squarespace also has a drag-and-drop feature that makes it easy to build your blog. Squarespace is easy to set up; it provides users with many options to build beautiful blogs with previous knowledge about programming and web development.

The tricky part about Squarespace is that its initial purpose was as a website platform for small business owners that were not good at coding or web development. Therefore, it is challenging to use it as a blogging platform. Most people start at Squarespace then move their platform to Word-Press.org.

Regardless, it has awesome-looking templates and themes that will make your blogsite look very attractive to your audience.

### Advantages of using Squarespace

- It is easy to set up a beautiful blog.
- You can use it for many activities, including an online eCommerce store for your products, your affiliate websites, and so much more.

### Disadvantages of using Squarespace

- Squarespace's initial development had websites in mind. Although you can use it for blogging, I wouldn't recommend picking it as your first choice.
- Blogs using the platform are slower than those using Ghost, Medium, and WordPress. Thus, they don't perform very well when it comes to SEO.
- The editor may be a little complex for a beginner blogger because it favors building pages, not blogs.

### How much Squarespace costs

Squarespace has two plans, i.e., personal plans, used mainly by bloggers, and a business plan.

The personal plan costs $16/month.

The business plan costs $26/month

### Squarespace is ideal for:

- Bloggers hoping to sell their products on their platform.

### Action step

As you have learned, there are many blogging platforms available on the internet today. Because it can be challenging to find what you need amidst all the chaos, choose something that correlates to your goals, and start setting up, which is the next step

### Setting up Your Blogging Platform

Since you know about the best platforms and have decided on the one to use, let's look at how you can set it up and start blogging right away. Below are the steps to setting up a blog.

**NOTE:** In this step, we shall focus on technical platforms like wordpress.org, wix.com, and ghost.org. Other platforms like Medium, Blogger, Tumblr, etc., are pretty straightforward. Just click on the site, and follow the prompts. Some platforms like Medium will only ask you for your email and then set up everything else for you.

Let's get started.

### Wordpress.org

Here's how to set up a WordPress blog:

### Step 1: Choose a domain name

The first step to setting up any blog is choosing your online address. Your online address is your domain name, the URL that someone will type to access your blog. For instance, karenfurnitures.com and bobelectronics.com are prime examples of domain names—you can use any other name that suits your blog.

When choosing a domain name, pay attention to the following considerations:

- It should be pronounceable. Pronounceable domain names are easy to remember and are less confusing to your audience.
- It should be simple and easy to type.
- You can use your name or go with your niche. For example, if your niche is metal works or do-it-yourself welding activities, you can go with tomwelding.com. It is simple, easy to remember, includes your niche, and is pronounceable.
- Keep your domain name short. If your domain name is straightforward and short, your audience will have an easy time writing it, and there will be very few instances of mistyping.
- Avoid using hyphens and numbers; only use letters. Other characters confuse people because they are such a hassle. Imagine telling someone to include an underscore, hyphen, and numbers when searching

for a blog. The chances are high that the person will forget the hyphen or the unique character you have included. It's better to keep things simple by using letters only.

- Never use another company's slogans, names, or style because you should be unique to gain authority. Secondly, using another company's slogan can get you reported, which can have dire consequences like delisting.
- Lastly, it should make sense; go for a domain name that users and search engines can understand.

### Step 2: Log in to the hosting platform you want to use

The most recommended hosting platform for wordpress.org is Bluehost.com. Visit Bluehost.com and type in the domain name you have chosen. Enter it in the filled provided and then click on search to see if it is available.

If your domain name is available, Bluehost will let you proceed with the getting-started process. If not, the domain name tool will suggest other domain names related to yours.

NOTE: In some instances, especially if you're a new user, BlueHost may give you a free domain name for a year.

## Step 3: Set up your hosting account

The Bluehost tools will ask you to enter some details before you finally set up your account. You will have to provide personal information, including your name, phone number, address, and how you would like to pay for the service.

You will also select some of the tools you would like to use.

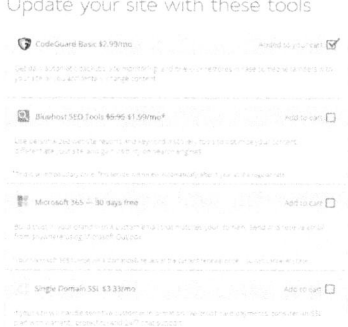

Enter the relevant information and check the appropriate boxes to complete setting up your account. Don't forget to read the terms of services and the cancellation policy. You should know what you are signing up for—don't accept things blindly.

Create a password for your hosting blog, and just like that, you will be all set.

### Step 4: Install wordpress.org

Once you create your hosting account, on the homepage dashboard, click on "My Sites" and then on "Create site." Enter all the basic information required, such as your email address, site name, tagline, etc.

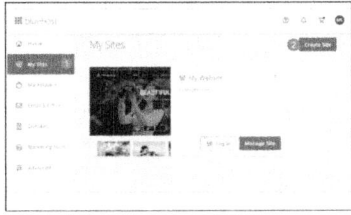

Once done, WordPress will start installing itself automatically. Once that process completes, go back to "My Sites" and log in to your WordPress blog.

### Step 5: Start customizing and writing your content

With WordPress installed on your blog, you can start blogging. Start by customizing your blog as you see fit—online tutorials will prove very helpful here—then move on to creating content for pages and blog posts. Your first blog post can be introducing your blog to your audience.

### Wix.com

To set up a wix.com site:

### Step 1

Type www.wix.com on your browser bar, then click on the big blue "Get started" button.

### Step 2

The platform will then ask you to either sign up with your Facebook account, Google, or email. Choose what works for you.

### *Step 3*

Click on "create a new site."

### *Step 4*

From here, everything else is easy. Wix will ask you about your niche, the features you want on your blog—for example, if you want to sell online, get subscribers, and create a blog. Check all of them and then continue.

## Does your website need any of the following features?

- ☑ Sell online
- ☑ Take bookings & appointments
- ☑ Get subscribers
- ☑ Create a blog

### Step 5

Pick a theme and then click on "build site." Wix will then build a site for you, a process that usually takes a few minutes.

### Step 6

Edit the details of the basic template provided. This basic platform is free.

## Step 7

At the bottom section of the free template provided, you will see 3 more options: "Pages," "Themes," and "More." Click on more, then click on "Upgrade" to select your domain name, register for self-hosting, and more.

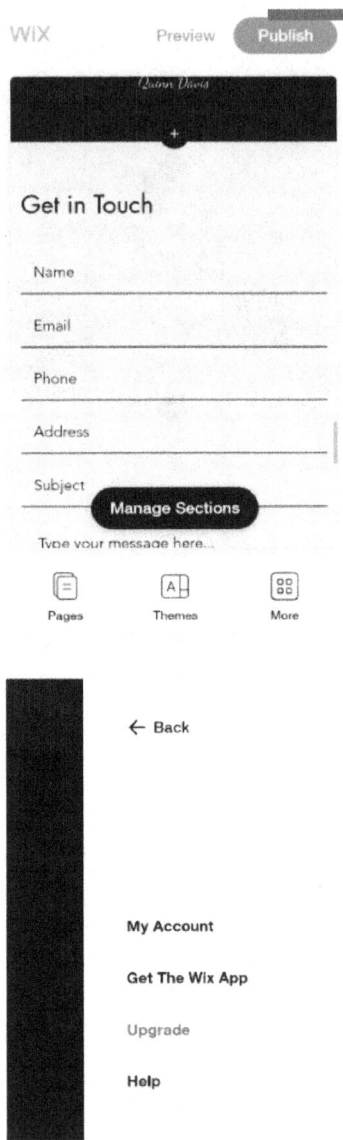

**Step 8**

Start blogging.

Everything is all set up now; start writing stories that you love.

### *Ghost.org*

To set up a ghost.org blog:

### Step 1: Buy a domain name

Just as is the case with Wordpress.org, you need a domain name to set up your Ghost blogging platform. You can get your domain name from any domain name provider such as iwantmyname, which offers a great service.

You can skip this step if you're using a hosting provider that also provides a domain name.

### Step 2: Get remote access tools for your blog

Ghost is entirely self-hosted. Therefore you will need remote access tools to run your server. You will need these tools to run commands and execute file operations like copying and moving things on your self-hosted platform.

For this step, you will download a piece of software called PuTTY to run commands and WinSCP to copy or move files.

If you're a Mac OS user, use a PuTTY alternative called Cyberduck. You can use Cyberduck to run commands and move, copy or paste files.

### Step 3: Obtain a hosting space

You will need hosting space on the internet. With Ghost, you can go with any hosting space you like. Some examples of hosting providers are Microsoft Azure, HostGator, Amazon AWS, GoDaddy, and DigitalOcean.

I would recommend DigitalOcean because it has a user-friendly interface and is much easier to set up for Ghost.

### Step 4: Add your domain name to your hosting provider of choice

It is now time to establish yourself online. Do this by adding/propagating your domain name on your hosting provider.

### Step 5: Change your Nameservers

By now, you have a server online that you can access remotely using PuTTY. What you have to do now is update the name of your server online with your remote server to make it much easier to transfer files and other things between your servers.

You can do this by simply updating the nameservers. All hosting providers have this feature. Just go to your hosting provider and find "update nameservers" on the dashboard.

### Step 6: Now prepare your server

Before you install Ghost, there are a few things you must get ready first. They include:

- Create a non-root user
  (https://m.youtube.com/watch?v=LbJK48gvXcA)
- Allow user permissions on your computer.
- Install Node.js (https://nodejs.org/en/).
- Install NGINX
  (https://docs.nginx.com/nginx/admin-
  guide/installing-nginx/installing-nginx-open-
  source/)
- Install MySQL
  https://dev.mysql.com/downloads/installer/
- Install Ghost CLI https://ghost.org/docs/ghost-cli/

**Step 7: Install Ghost**

Install Ghost on your server. Here is a Ghost.org guide on how to install the Ghost blogging platform

https://ghost.org/docs/install/

Make sure that Ghost is running perfectly with its default theme. If you don't like the default theme, you can go to the Ghost marketplace to get more elegant-looking, free themes.

**Step 8: Add a comment section**

The Ghost blogging platform doesn't have inbuilt comment features; you will have to install one for your platform. Some good ones include Commento and Isso.

You can install more items on your server like Google Analytics to manage and analyze your blogs, but everything we have covered so far should be enough to get you started blogging.

With your blog running and content consistently published,

you will see some traffic trickling in. At that point, you need to optimize your blog for more traffic. More traffic means more audience, more customers or clients, and more authority on the internet. Let's discuss how to do that in the next chapter:

## 3

## GETTING YOUR BLOG NOTICED (HOW TO GROW TRAFFIC TO YOUR BLOG)

Your blog is of no value if people can't see it. People/audience are everything when it comes to making money from a blog.

It doesn't matter what kind of business you have; if you have a significant following, you have 70% of what you need to make money. The remaining 30% is all about content marketing and audience nurturing.

A blog is the best way to reach people. According to Opt-in Monster statistics, 77% of internet users read blogs, with users reading over 20 billion blog pages per month. Even marketers and businesses know this. The same statistics show that businesses that blog get 97% more links to their eCommerce store, which is why many people today are investing in blogs.

Furthermore, people refer to blogs for almost everything before they partake in whichever activity they would like to do. For example, before you go to the gym or try a new diet or recipe, you will Google it first to get some background information first.

Additionally, before buying anything, be it a movie, online service, a product, song, just about anything, you have to Google it first to see what bloggers are saying about it before you spend your money. In a recent study by GE Capital Retail Bank, researchers determined that 81% of people research something before committing to a purchase.

In a nutshell, blogging is a powerful asset to anyone looking to make money online. However, it can only be powerful if people read it and engage with it.

Let's discuss practical approaches you can use to get your blog noticed:

## Leverage Social Media Marketing To Drive Traffic To Your Blog

Social media is one of the best places to generate traffic to your blog. Today, more than half of the earth's population is on social media. Social media has connected us to people worldwide and allowed us to reach many people. The best part is that you can get these people to visit your website without trying so hard.

Here is how you can move traffic from your social media site to your blogging site.

### Fill your profile

Your social media profile is the first thing people see when they come across your social media page. Places like Facebook About section, Twitter bio, LinkedIn page, etc., paint a picture of who you are and what you are about to your audience.

Therefore, you should take advantage of your profile; use it to talk about your blog and include a link that directs your audience to your blog.

Ensure you create an account on popular social media platforms, making sure to include a description of your blog and a backlink to the blog on each platform.

### Welcome new followers

Whenever you get a new follower, welcome them with a good appreciation message. Greet them, thank them for following you, follow them back, then introduce them to your blog. This strategy works every time.

When someone feels seen and value, it makes you seem friendly and social, which helps nurture a relationship that makes it easier to nurture and convert contacts and leads. When you nurture relationships, a simple task like clicking on a link that will lead them to your blog won't meet too much internal resistance.

You can even go further to show your new followers how they can benefit from reading your blogs. For instance, if you blog about body transformations, keeping fit, and staying healthy through exercises, you can encourage your new follower to visit your blog to see how they can achieve that.

Social media is a social place; therefore, be friendly, communicate, be helpful and socialize as much as you can. Doing that will give you visibility, which will help drive traffic to your blog.

.  .  .

## Optimize your social media with visuals

When people visit your social media pages, it should inspire them and leave them curious to learn more about you. One way to do this is by using visuals on your social media pages. People love pictures, videos, and other visual content formats like infographics. That's why platforms like Instagram, Snapchat, and Tiktok are so popular today.

To take advantage of this, add beautiful but relevant pictures/gifs/videos to your blog and make sure you can preview the visuals on your social media pages. If people can get interested in the visual content you post on your social media page, they will visit your blog to get more similar content.

## Make your content easy to share

The first rule to blogging is to make it possible for your audience to share your content. As a blogger, your audience is one of your best marketing channels.

If a person tells their best friend or family to visit a blog, there are very high chances that they will visit that blog because it's much easier to trust someone you already know, and you will also feel like you owe them for reading that blog.

You know how disappointing it could be if your best friend tells you to read or do something they are passionate about, but you don't. You can turn that feeling on to your audience.

Always encourage your audience to share your content with their friends on social media. Include a quick backlink that will take them to their social media pages for sharing.

Various blog tools can allow you to do this with ease. One such tool is AddThis, which is very effective and completely free. Another commonly used by blogs hosted on word-press.org is Cresta Social Share Counter, a plugin you will install on your WordPress blog. These tools make sharing on Facebook, Twitter, LinkedIn, Pinterest, Google Plus, Reddit, WhatsApp, Telegram, Tumblr, and more much easier.

You can also include "Click to Tweet" on your blog, making it easy for your audience to share your phrases and part of your content with their Twitter followers. The tweet will contain a link to your blog, encouraging Twitter followers to visit your blog, thus increasing how much traffic your blog gets.

Enabling sharing is similar to having brand ambassadors or influencers of your blog—who are free.

### Always engage with your audience

As a tool, social media makes it possible to engage directly with people in real-time. It is the fastest way of interacting with your audience, and thus, you can get feedback or reviews on your blog that you can act on quickly.

For example, if you got some information wrong, your audience can reach you through your social media page quicker, enabling you to correct it before too many people see it.

Besides getting feedback, you can also engage with your social media target audience to drive traffic to your blog. You can do this through the following ways:

- **Participate in chats:** This can be on any platform. Visit any social media platform and search for a topic you can contribute to constructively. Find chats and questions and participate in answering them. Do this consistently to a point where people on the chat will see you as an authority in that particular field. Your authority will encourage people to click on your profile to find out more about you, or they will follow you.

- **Respond to any comments about your blog or niche:** If someone mentions your blog or you in a comment, never fail to engage with that user, which is something most bloggers don't do. They ignore a comment mentioning them, thinking it is just one person, but what they fail to realize is that many people are waiting for you to answer that one casual follower. They probably had the same question and seeing that another person has asked it, they will wait to see your reply through that person. Therefore, even if you don't have a firm grasp of the question, engage with that person and ask for clarification or more information. Doing this will give you a good reputation as a blogger. As a plus, such questions will provide you with an opportunity to showcase your value or what you can do for your audience.
- **Leverage hashtags:** Use hashtags when posting content on your social media pages and engage with other people that use hashtags within your niche. A majority of people on social media search for information using hashtags. If you happen to be using one, your page will be part of the search results.

### Contribute to relevant forums

Several online communities or groups interact through sharing knowledge. For instance, if I would like to know something or get some clarification, I will post the question on a relevant forum, and people there will answer my question—some even go further to provide a link to where I can find the answer.

The best places to find such forums are Reddit, Quora, Inbound.org, and StumbleUpon. You can also use Facebook and Instagram Groups.

People on these platforms are in it for knowledge. They are willing and prepared to learn, share knowledge, and interact with people whose interests match theirs.

You can find the most engaged traffic from such people because, unlike other social media platforms where the audience is looking for entertainment, people on these forums are looking to learn anything new and share their knowledge on a specific topic or niche. By contributing to discussions within your niche, you can introduce your blog. You can summarize an answer to the question asked, then tell people to visit your website to get a deeper and broader answer. You can also build authority on these platforms.

When people see that you are more engaged and know more about topics in a particular niche, they will be curious about you. They will visit your profile to see what you are about, and when they get there, they will find a link to your blog, leading to more traffic to your blog.

As a blogger, the primary goal behind everything you do on social media platforms should be to drive traffic to your blog. Thus, ensure that most of your posts and social media engagements include a backlink to your blog.

. . .

## Make friends with influencers

Some people have a large following that listens to them and hangs on their every word and recommendation. We call these people influencers. Influencers are highly trusted and held in such high esteem by their audience that when they say a product or a service is good, people will believe it and buy the product there and then.

Influencers wield this power because they have spent most of their time building their reputation and trust among their followers. For example, if you are a bodybuilder and Dwayne "The Rock" Johnson tells you that a certain supplement is the best for achieving more muscle gain, you will buy that supplement, trusting that it is the best supplement.

You will do that because he has results to show for it (massive muscles) and because he has been doing bodybuilding for so long, with many people witnessing his bodybuilding progress. The same goes for fashion influencers like Kendall Jenner or makeup influencers like James Charles.

If you want to get fast and easy traffic, find an influencer in your niche, someone you know commands a significant following or audience. This person can be a blogger like you or even your competitor. Make friends with influencers and encourage them to mention your blog on their posts on social media or in their blogs.

Besides driving traffic, influencers can help you build your brand quicker. They will shorten the time it would take you to build authority in your niche. They will help you reach a new market or even make people previously uninterested in your blog interested in it. Influencers can help you rebuild trust with former audiences or customers that stopped reading your blogs or buying products that you sell on your blog.

## Try paid social advertising

Your social media posts can only reach your followers, social media friends, and the people with whom your audience shares your content. Sometimes these people are not enough. On other occasions, some of them will not even visit your blog, no matter how great your posts are.

In such a situation, you should expand your reach to find more people interested in your posts. Paid social media advertising is the best way to do this.

Social media paid advertising knows no boundaries. Your content can reach just about anyone in wherever location they may be. These people are not necessarily your followers or people that have heard about you before. They are strangers that may be interested in what you have on your social media page or blog.

Social media platforms like Facebook, Instagram, and Twitter use algorithms that can predict the type of people that might be interested in your content. You can also specifically direct your content to specific people.

For instance, if you know that most of your audience are females aged 25 to 35, you can tell the social media advertisers to target this demographic specifically. You can also target an audience within a specific region, nationality, religion, and anything else.

Paid advertising is an effective way to drive traffic to your blog. The best part is that paid social media ads are not all that expensive. For example, Facebook and Instagram—owned by the same company—cost an average of $0.50 to $2.00 per click. YouTube video ads cost an average of $o.1 to $0.3 per view. And you know as well as I do that if someone takes their time to click on your ad or watch a video, they are truly interested in what you are offering. Therefore, it will be easy for you to turn them into loyal audiences for your blog.

### Action step

Social media is one of the best traffic sources. People enjoy social media; it is somewhat addictive; therefore, be certain that almost all your audience is on social media—statistics show that 83.36% of internet users are active on social media.

Create accounts on all social media platforms and forums, and start working on driving traffic to your blog. If things are working well and you need a little boost, you can sign up for paid advertising.

### Using Email Marketing To Drive Traffic To Your Blog

Social media and influencer marketing are great ways to drive traffic to your blog. No one can dispute that they work exceptionally well. However, it's important not to forget a traditional, effective way to drive engaging traffic to your blog: email.

According to statistics by Hubspot, email generates $38 for every $1 spent on marketing. That is a 3800% Return on Investment, making email marketing one of the best ways to drive traffic to your blog or market your business.

According to McKinsey & Company, a global management consulting firm, email beats social media 40 times in customer acquisition.

As you can tell, email marketing is very effective when it comes to driving targeted traffic to your blog or acquiring new customers. However, it can only work if you do it right.

Let's look at some tips you can use to make the most out of email marketing.

### Tip 1: Build a list

You can't just throw emails left and right, hoping that people will read them and take action. It doesn't work that way. That's akin to fishing in a swimming pool. Your best bet is to ensure that the people receiving your emails are interested in reading them or, at the least, open to reading them.

The people who make the best contacts are your loyal followers, customers—people who have bought something from your blog before—, leads, and people who happen to land on your blog once or even twice. These people are sure bets.

They have shown some interest before on your blog, so the likelihood is high that they will revisit your site when they receive your email. When sending your emails, make it simple for them to reach your site: it should be dummy-simple to get to your blog from your email.

That brings us to a very key question: how do you create an email list?

Have a sleek, concise and simple signup form on your blog. This form should be easy to find, understand, and use. Something that will take seconds of your readers' time to get done with—signing up to your newsletter- should not be a nuisance for users because they visit your blog to read your content, not sign-up forms.

You can have your sing up form in the sidebar or footer, but the most recommended format is to have it as a popup, roughly 5-10 seconds after someone has visited your blog or when they are leaving your blog—we call these exit popups. You can also have it embedded in your posts.

Pop-ups make it easy, quick, and convenient for your visitors to share their email information or subscribe to your newsletters while reading through your content or browsing your site. Ensure that this pop-up quickly disappears once users have submitted their contact information.

### Tips on building a great popup form

- **Make a compelling offer:** Your audience won't feel compelled to give up their email information if there is nothing in it for them. Think about it. Can you give out your email address to a site if there is nothing good in it for you? Of course not! Therefore, you must give people a reason to sign up for your forms. Think about what your audience might want —something you can give them for free. For example, you can give a free eBook, software, a report, an offer on what you are selling on your blog, free shipping, trial, sample, etc. Anything you can think of that your audience would find valuable and want to have will do fine. Make this benefit as clear as possible on the headline. The headline should be bold and very compelling—audiences should tell what they'll get in exchange for their email.

Below the headline, include a short but clear description of the headline and the popup's purpose. One mistake that most bloggers make is packing a lot of information on their popup emails. Please don't do this. Instead, get straight to the point. One sentence or two is enough to pass your message.

- **You can also include a good image on your popup:** Capitalize on the power of visuals. A beautiful image showing the benefits users stand to gain from signing up to your newsletter can stop the visitor from hurriedly overlooking the popup. When you use visuals, it'll increase your sign-up conversion rate.
- **Make the form very simple:** Ask only for the email because this is what you are targeting. You can also ask for a first name, but don't make the sign-up form overly complex. A simple form takes a short time to fill, encouraging visitors to sign up.
- **Optimize your popup emails for mobile phones**: A majority of people access the internet on their mobile phones. Thus, ensure your pop-up forms will look great on mobile devices as they would on computers. Besides, a large percentage of people check their emails on their mobile phones. Therefore, when you send them an email that will redirect them to your site, they will visit it through their mobile phones. Thus, it is imperative to optimize your blog for smartphones—we shall look at this further when talking about SEO.
- **Employ gamification:** Some popups are interactive. They include gamification like "spin the wheel to select your offer" right after the user has submitted their emails. One statistic shows that popups with gamification have a 12.74% sign-up rate than the basic sign-up format. As much as people are always

in a hurry, they like to play simple games. Out of curiosity, they will spin the wheel to see what they will get.

Below is an example of a good popup.

### How to build great pop-ups

Here're some ideas guaranteed to help you build outstanding newsletter popups.

- **Design your form:** The first step to building a popup is to think about which design suits your audience best. Your design should include a headline, tagline, a form with a field to enter the name and email address, and an image. Make it unique, catchy, and elegant.
- **Decide when you want the pop-up to appear:** When do you want your pop to show up? Most popups show up immediately after a person lands on the blog, 5-10 minutes after landing on the site, when they are leaving, or when a user scrolls down the site. What you choose will depend entirely on how well you know your audience. For instance, if most of your audience spends a little more time on your blog, you can create a delayed popup—5 seconds after

landing on your page). If your audience doesn't like interruptions when reading your website, have the popup appear when someone is navigating away from your blog. If you want your audience to read and enjoy your content before asking them to sign up, you can go with the scroll-triggered popup.

- **Promote your other blog posts using popups:** If a particular blog post you made in the past received great interaction and engagement, use a popup to redirected readers to that blog post. Popular content increases traffic. If you would like to do this, you should consider one key thing: use an exit-intent popup. You don't want to interrupt someone when they are midway through reading content with a pop-up that takes them to another content. It doesn't feel right. Instead, tailor your popup to show up when the reader has scrolled down to 80-90% of that page, with a text saying, "Have you seen this?" then include a link to take them to that page.

- **Tailor your popups to a specific page:** Your popups should not appear just anywhere; if they do, they will seem out of place. Take an example where you have a DIY blog and a post taking about steps to fixing a broken window, but a pop-up about cooking or fixing a quick meal on the go appears on that post. It will seem out of place; too generic. If you are talking about fixing a broken window, users should see a popup with offers related to fixing a broken window. Such "out of place" popups come about due to poor designs or by making them too generic. They will look bad to your audience.

On the other hand, perfectly tailored popup ads will increase your subscription rate because they are relevant to the user, making signing up more compelling.

You can use these tips to build pop-up email forms for Mailchimp, Sitecontrol, Unbounce, and Wishpond.

Besides your blog, you can also collect contacts from your followers on social media. You can create a social media ad that encourages people to sign up with their emails. After, you can use those emails that you have gathered for email marketing.

**Tip 2: Start sending emails**

Once you get yourself a list—that's the easy part—start sending your readers emails.

Besides sending your emails, ensure that your subscribers will open your emails and read through them until they take action. To achieve this, you have to stand out among all your competitors, including all the other emails your customer or prospect receives. You need to connect with them and encourage them to take action.

How can you do this?

Here are tips to help you master this facet of email marketing:

**Use a subject line that will get them hooked on the spot**

Your email subject line directly determines if your audience will open and read that email; it's the bread and butter of your email marketing campaign. Therefore, you must come up with a catchy and compelling subject line.

A good subject line should be concise and direct to the point —you can also include a call-to-action. Remember, you need to stand out among everybody else in the inbox. Therefore, it would be wise to use marketing strategies like creating a fearful state of disbelief, a sense of urgency, asking an intriguing question, or start with the benefit your audience will get from answering that email.

For instance, I received an email from an eCommerce business saying, "Have you looked at this yet?"—using a question. I was curious to look at the new stock and products—hoping that something I had been waiting for and couldn't find before was in the new stock.

I got one from Amazon.com saying, "Today Only: Top deals $0.99 and up…" Giving a sense of urgency—for only today, I could get a good product for as low as $0.99, let me jump on it quick. Another one from Amazon also started with a benefit; it said, *"Up to 80% off select…"*

There was also one from Copyblogger saying, "So, this is goodbye…" – using a fearful state of disbelief strategy. Copybloggers was not closing; they were renewing their email list. But, if you read that subject line, you might think that they were shutting down.

Do an A/B split test to see which strategy works and stick with it. An A/B split test compares two or more different versions to see which one works best.

### Action step

Depending on your email body, find a way to use these subject lines but customize them to your target audience.

### Make sure the body will lead to the call-to-action

When you use a subject line that is catchy enough to compel your reader to click through to your email, it will spark their interest. The question is: will the content in the email make them respond to your call-to-action? Your readers should visit your blog after reading the body.

A tip used by successful bloggers to increase their email conversion rate is to converse with their readers as if they were their friends while still being as professional as possible. Write your email body as if you are talking with that person offline; connect with them, create good relationships, then invite them to visit your blog.

You need to know a bit more about your readers to connect with them. It is important to know the kind of readers your get for your blog. Knowing your audience will make it a lot easier to write for them.

Use "You" and "Me" when talking to your readers. Talk to them as you would a friend. Deepen the relationship, but don't come off as too casual. Keep it professional.

**Personalize your text**

Another important factor to include in your emails is keeping them personalized. By this, I mean you should include the name of the person you are sending the email to. You can also include other personal details if you know a thing or two about your reader. However, don't include so much personal information that you end up looking like a stalker. Have just enough to capture their attention, something that will make them feel like you know and value them.

This is important because statistics from Bluecore found that personalized emails had a 139% increase in click-through rate compared to static, regular emails. Bluecore collected this data from over 3.26 billion emails sent by marketers.

Mailchimp and Wishpond sites will help you personalize your emails before you send them, but you can also do this manually using a spreadsheet.

## Segment your emails

Once you have an email list, you will find that you have a different category of readers. Some of them will be beginners, others regular readers, and some will be your most loyal readers. You might want to have a different email writing style mails for beginners and loyal readers.

Beginners are new and will want you to spend more time crafting compelling emails. In contrast, your regular and loyal readers can respond to a simple email like "Here is new content for you."

It's in your best interest to segment your email for the different categories or groups in your email list. Although the email content will differ, the landing page should be the same for all of them—unless you have intimate knowledge of what your audience wants and are sure a different page can offer that and lead to higher conversion.

## Include a clear call to action—vital

You have to make it clear what you want your reader to do before and after reading through your email, which, in this case, is to visit your blog.

Starting from your subject line, encourage your reader to click through the email to find out more. Once they click through, include another call to action in the body that will make them visit your site.

Make it easy for them to take these calls to action. Most marketers use a clear colored button embedded within the email body. When readers click on these buttons, they quickly get redirected to a specific article or page on the blog.

If you want to create these clear call-to-action buttons for your emails, use formatting sites like Mailchimp, Wishpond, and Fusion. You can learn more about that from the following resource:

https://themeforest.net/item/fusion-metro-email-news-letter-template/4000633

### Create visual newsletters

As mentioned earlier, people love visual content; it helps capture their attention and keeps them interested for longer. If your email is image-rich and teasing more such images in the blog, people will feel more motivated to click through the "read more" button that leads them to your blog.

### Monitor your click-through times to figure out when (time) a majority of your readers open their mails

Even though we are all busy with our jobs, education, businesses, etc., at some point during the day, we get time to browse through our emails and click on sites. As someone looking to drive traffic to your blog, you should note when your readers are more willing to click through to your emails, then schedule to send your emails during these times.

Emails get into the inbox in reverse chronological order, with the latest emails appear on top and the older ones appear below. When you log into your email account, you are more likely to click on the email at the top before you scroll down. If you schedule your emails to when your readers are likely to open their email accounts, you will appear on top, increasing the chances of email subscribers reading your email.

Sending emails at random times is counterproductive, no matter how good the email is. Sometimes people are in a rush and won't take time to read through all the emails in one sitting; they will filter out the important ones and ignore the rest. If your email is at the top, featuring a catchy subject line, you will get a click-through.

## Action step

99% of people that visit a blog for the first time are not in there to buy whatever you are selling on your site—no matter how much you want them to buy. However, 75% of these people are likely to revisit your site to take up your Call-to-Action.

A call-to-action is what you want people to do, for example, clicking and making purchases through your affiliate links, buying items from your site, or subscribing to your services. Email is the best way to encourage people to come back—it's the best way to nurture leads.

Email marketing is a permission-based method to drive traffic or to market yourself. People have willingly submitted their emails to you—meaning it won't be such a nuisance for them to receive your emails.

Create an email list NOW and start nurturing these email subscribers with compelling emails.

## Uing Search Engine Optimization To Drive Traffic to Your Blog

Another way to ensure your get noticed is to appear on search engine results pages (SERPs) for your target/niche keywords. Search engine optimization is one of the most important ways to ensure that you get qualified traffic to your blog. That's because:

Unlike social media and email marketing, people searching for specific keywords have already decided which information they want. They haven't been coerced or motivated; instead, they are actively looking for you—or your content.

Now:

The internet has countless tips on optimizing your blog for SEO. While most of them—at least those from trusted sources—work, some fundamental SEO principles that will never change and optimizing for them can make all the difference. We shall focus on those fundamentals, but before we do, let's define SEO.

Search Engine Optimization (SEO) is a way of optimizing your blog—and its contents—to rank highly on the Search Engine Results Page for targeted keywords.

When someone from anywhere in the world uses a search engine to search for keywords related to your content, SEO ensures that your content appears on the first page results.

Having defined SEO, here are SEO techniques you can use to ensure that your content ranks on the first page of SERP:

**Make your site fast**

I can't stress this enough: *site speed is a vital SEO aspect.*

In the early 2000s, you could get away with sites that load slowly as long as you knew you have something good to offer. Today, it is tough to stand a chance or ranking if your site loads slowly. Site speed is now an important ranking factor that supersedes a sleek design or content quality.

Even if we put aside Google's speed requirements, a slow site speed is very frustrating. Often, people will get discouraged when a site loads slowly, abandon it, and move on to the next one that responds much faster.

Here's the reality:

Data reality from eConsultancy found that 40% of people abandon a site that takes more than 3 seconds to load. Most people think that a slow site is somewhat untrustworthy and might even refrain from buying anything from such a site.

What should you do to enhance your page load speed?

- First, eliminate all elements that might slow down your site. For example, if you have redundant plugins that you're not using—assuming you're using the wordpress.org platform—or a widget, remove it from your site or avoid adding it in the first place.
- Remove too many ads. Although they can help you make money, too many ads are the number one cause of a high bounce rate—bounce rate is when someone lands on your site and leaves without doing anything. Too many ads make your site load very slowly.
- Test the theme you are using to see if it affects your loading speeds. Some themes will slow down your site.
- Don't use too many high-resolution images. Even though images are one of the best ways to grab attention and keep audiences on your site, using large images with giant graphics might take a lot more time to load.
- If you have a sidebar on your pages with unnecessary information and items, take them out, and replace them with only essential widgets. Just keep your site simple and relevant to the user. Users want a simple, beautiful site that is informative. Period!

Once you've done all this, perform a site speed test to see how you are performing. Here are tools you can use:

Lighthouse: https://developers.google.com/web/tools/lighthouse/

Pingdom: https://tools.pingdom.com/

GTmetrix: https://gtmetrix.com/

Ubersuggest: https://neilpatel.com/ubersuggest/

The general rule of thumb is to ensure that your site loads in less than 3 seconds—shoot for a 1-2 second load speed.

## Link to other sites with quality content

Linking with other websites is very important in SEO because it gives your blog backlinks that improve your authority. Google and other search engines pay significant attention to backlinks when determining where to rank a website on their index. Backlinking creates "trackable traffic," making your blog look more resourceful and valuable to search engines.

Besides, if you link to another site with relevant content, you are making it easy for your readers to get other quality content, thus improving your user experience. Even if a blogger is your direct competitor, but he/she has high-quality content that you think your reader can use, link to them. You can ask them to link back to you.

People with authoritative sites will be more willing to link back to you if you link to their content first. Just notify them when you link to them; they might love your posts and link back to you as well—or share it with their audience, thus driving traffic to your blog.

However, since the idea is to link back to other sites, you must ensure you link back to sites that offer the best value and are authoritative. Linking to low-quality sites is counter-productive: it will make you look bad.

Search engines will not favor you when you link back to poor quality sites or sites that don't adhere to Google guidelines. For instance, linking to a site that shows graphic content or full of ads will not favor you in any way.

### Be human in your posts

Sometimes bloggers get caught up trying to include keywords in every sentence or paragraph to their content. They work so hard to get noticed by search engines that they forget to be human in the process. Do your best to avoid this practice.

Content manipulated for search engines can be difficult to read or understand, even when it ranks first on Google. Search engines won't buy what you are selling on your blog; they won't share your content with their friends or do anything else that your actual audience—loyal ones—can do.

Therefore, be human. Let your content engage and connect with people; bloggers that put readers first will always prosper. For example, Brian Clarks' Copyblogger is a multi-million dollar digital marketing company because they always put readers first. They are passionate about giving their readers the best reading experience. Their content is simple to read and understand, informative, no ads all over, and is very engaging. Reading their content will prove this.

If you want to be a successful blogger in the long term like Brian Clark, write for people first before you think about search engines.

You can do this by creating content that people will find valuable and helpful. Forget about search engines, SEO, and everything else when writing. Just focus on offering something valuable.

Funny enough, Google and other search engines will reward you for this. Today, Google algorithms pay great attention to content quality—hence the phrase, "Content is King."

When your readers know that you publish high-quality, valuable content, they will always look for you, trust you, and share your work. It won't take much to convince them to buy using your affiliate links. Furthermore, other bloggers will be less reluctant to link to you.

### Encourage good sites to link to you

In real life, it is much easier to trust people with good friends than a loner. Google, Bing, and other search engines also think the same. If a site has a connection with other trustworthy, high-quality sites, it shows them that your blog is also valuable.

Every blogger knows that linking to sites with good content will make them look good. Before you ask other people to link to you, make sure that your blog, from your page loading speeds to content, is great. Blogging is your business. Thus, invest your time, money, and other resources to ensure that every aspect is perfect.

Even though bloggers spend an average of 4 hours on a blog, most dedicate a lot more time to ensuring that their content matches their audience needs and is search engine friendly.

Work hard on your blog too, and when it is perfect, encourage other bloggers with quality blogs to link to you.

### Use keywords wisely

Keywords are words or phrases in your content that people search for on their search engine search bar. Consider this example:

"Making money blogging requires that you build a good quality blog before your start monetizing, using the following technique..." If this is a part of a paragraph on your blog, your site will come up when someone searches for *"making money blogging"* on their search engine.

Keywords are a key part of SEO. We can go as far as saying that without keywords, it's impossible to rank on search engines. After all, how will the search engine know that your content is what a user is looking for without some related words or phrases?

However, although keywords are integral to driving organic traffic to your blog, do not stuff your content with keywords. Search engines like Google have algorithms that can notice blogs trying to take advantage of keywords to improve their rankings. When Google realizes that your content is of poor quality, but with keywords everywhere, it may penalize you.

Remember, your priority should be quality content, then after delivering that, edit it by including relevant keywords to boost your rankings. One or two keywords per article should do.

Also, use long-tail keywords. Here is an example from a search on "best SEO tips" vs. "best SEO tips for beginner bloggers using WordPress."

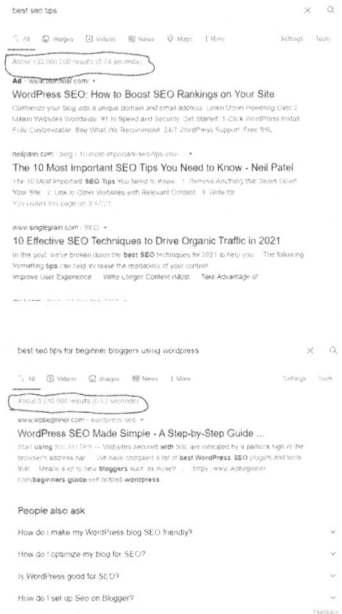

The first search parameter, "best SEO tips," has 133 million results, and in these results, highly authoritative blogs that have been around for years are dominating the results. Thus, to appear on the first page for these keywords, you must outrank 133 million sites.

On the other hand, the second search using long-tail keywords only has 5 million results, and not so many authoritative sites ranking for it. Most of the sites ranking for these keywords have poor quality content that you can [possible] outrank with easy if you create high-quality content coupled with an effective backlinking strategy.

Therefore, you stand a better chance of appearing on the first page of SERP when you use long-tail keywords than when using short-tail keywords. You can use the same strategy when bidding for ads later on when selling your products on your blog—hot tip: use ads with long-tail keywords; they are cheaper, and you stand a better chance of converting.

Another reason why targeting long-tail keywords trumps targeting short-term ones is that they are very specific. Take the example of "Best SEO tips for a beginner blogger using WordPress" vs. "best SEO tips." The former shows you that the users know what they want and are likely to buy a tool/eBook, subscribe to your lessons, or engage with you. The latter may be just trying to learn what SEO is or how it works—they are not ready to take any serious action.

When starting a blog and building traffic, it would be wise to use long-tail keywords. After you have gained enough authority, you can go for short-tail keywords.

**How to find keywords**

- Think of a topic or a question you are interested in talking about, then search for it on the Google search engine. Scroll down to the bottom of the result page to find, "Searches related to…" section. You will find a couple of long-tail keywords you can use in your content.
- Brainstorm to find some keywords you think your audience might use to find your content based on your niche. Come up with a long list, then narrow it down to the most effective ones.
- In your previous post, look at your comment section to find the questions that your audience asks. Gather a couple of suggestions for your next post.
- Use Google autocomplete recommendations. You have probably used this feature multiple times already. When you are typing in a query on Google's

search bar, Google will usually auto-complete your questions for you. As a blogger, you should note these autosuggestions because they are directly from Google, the search engine that will broadcast your site to your users.

- Once you have gathered a couple of keywords that you think are the best of the best in your list, use a keyword research tool to see how effective they are. Keyword tools tell you the best alternatives for your keywords with the search volume for that keyword. Long-tail keywords will have a much lower volume.
- A keyword research tool like Ubersuggest has a reputation for helping online marketers find the best long-tail versions of the key phrases you are thinking of using. It also shows you the competition level on that suggested keyword, the clicks you might get, and the monthly search volume.

Other good keyword tools to are:

- Keywordtool.io, which uses Google autocomplete suggestions for your keywords.
- Soovle finds and collects keywords from other authoritative websites like eBay, Amazon, YouTube, Ask.com, Wikipedia, etc. They also collect suggestions from the leading search engines.
- Use the Google search console to find keywords you already rank for, then optimize that content or article to appear on the first page of SERPs.
- Google Trends is another hot spot to find keywords. Google Trends uses news headlines, trends, and other algorithms to determine if your keyword will garner more interest or not in the future. Enter your keyword on the search bar and click on the search

button. The platform will show you an "Interest over Time graph" that will tell you how your keyword will perform in the future.

Here is an example: A projection of a keyword, "The Grammys," which is up-trending.

"The Royals" keyword is projected to fall

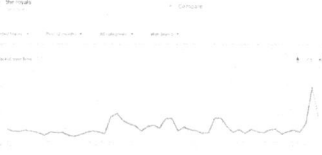

## Optimize your URLs

Your URLs also play an essential role when it comes to ranking. The general rule of thumb is to keep your URLs shorter, cleaner, and more readable to give your users and search engines an easier time.

If humans can find it challenging to read or write down your URL, search engine bots will also struggle. For example, consider the following URL:

https://www.farmersblog.blogpost.com/en=us?id&+f=bvfjr-bvfjhbvj346315643513fgafea/

A URL like this is terrible and will cost you SEO juice. For one, it is too long and has so many characters—what's the purpose of &id, =, +, etc.—It also doesn't give a brief preview of what your blog is about, and it doesn't have a keyword.

In contrast, consider the following URL

https://www.farmersblog.com/article/6543543/

This URL is also not great because it doesn't tell users and search engines what to expect from the blog. Furthermore, it doesn't contain any keywords.

Now consider the following URL:

https://www.farmersblog.com/5-ways-to-grow-beetroot/

Such an URL spot on for your readers and search engine bots. It is simple, clearly explains what the post is all about, has keywords, and doesn't contain so many different characters. Besides, it is easier to remember.

As much as such engines are robots, they need guidance to make the ranking process much simpler. Google rewards bloggers that give their bots an easier time.

Some expert bloggers from copyblogger.com suggest that only 2 to 4 keywords should be in the URL to make it easy for your readers to memorize.

Other URL tips you should pay attention to are:

- Use hyphens (-) instead of (_) or just combining a sentence as one word. Google algorithm can read hyphens but not underscores.
- Avoid using capital letters; they are confusing both to humans and search engines. It is hard to remember

where you placed a capital letter and where you
didn't.

- If you have always been using
  https://www.yoururl.com, don't get to a point where
  you change it to https://yoururl.com. Search engines
  will consider these URL iterations different sites.
  Stick to one format.
- Include your best keywords or phrases in your URLs.

### Add Meta descriptions

A meta description is a summary of what is within your blog.
It describes what's is in your article. Many search users read
meta descriptions before they decide that the blog is worth
reading. Take this example

Your Meta descriptions should contain around 160 characters or less.

Search engines will show your Meta descriptions on the
results page, encouraging users to click on your site. The
more people click on your site, the higher you will rank on
SERP.

### Action step

To add Meta tags, scroll down your blog edit screen page and find the All-in-one SEO (AIO-SEO) meta box.

### Implement Schema Markup

Schema markup is very critical for your Google ranking. Schema markup is a code that you generate to help the Google engine quickly crawl and analyze your content. Crawling is the process by which Google looks for and updates new content for people to find.

Schema markup enables you to explain to Google the different parts of your content. It breaks down your content into different parts so that it's much easier for Google to feature your article in featured snippets—we shall discuss featured snippets shortly.

Implement schema markup is a free and easy process. To get started, go to Structured Data Markup Helper:

https://www.google.com/webmasters/markup-helper/

Since you are blogging, click on articles.

Then copy the URL with the article you want to markup and past it in the box under the lists.

Then click on "Start Tagging."

You will see a page like this.

Mark everything up like this

Add the name, author and everything, date published, etc. Then click on "Create HTML."

Replace your core source code with the newly HTML generated, and you will be all set.

### Try to get the featured snippet on SERPs

Featured snippets are a core Google search feature. Google has been working hard to make it easier for users to find the answers they are looking for as quickly as possible.

To meet this goal, they introduced "featured snippets" into their search results. These snippets contain answers for the queries that users are interested in. Featured snippets come as a paragraph, list, or table, and they usually appear on top or below the first result.

# 4

## HOW TO MONETIZE YOUR BLOG AND MAKE MONEY BLOGGING

One of the advantages of starting a blog is that you can use it to make money. Even if you are a passionate or hobby blogger doing it for fun or the love of it, there's nothing wrong with making a couple of bucks from your blog.

In this chapter, we shall take a deeper look at some of the best ways to monetize your blog and make money from blogging. Implementing just a few of the techniques we shall discuss in this chapter is enough to help you generate a few hundred if not thousands of dollars in income per month.

Let's get started:

### Sponsored Posts: Making Money through Brand Partnerships

Sponsored posts are articles you write and get paid for by sponsors—as the name suggests.

A brand or business may ask you to talk about their brand, products, or services, then pay you a good amount of money for it—this will be a brand or company selling products within your niche.

Your sponsor or client may be looking to reach a new audience—your readers—and may ask you to write about their products/services or brand and post it on your blog. Then, you will include some backlinks that will lead readers back to the sponsor's website to buy the talked about product/service.

Sponsored posts can take many forms like:

- A sponsor can ask you to write about a new discount, offers, giveaways, or other promotions on sponsored products.
- A sponsor may also ask you to give a thorough review of a product or service and post it on your blog.
- A sponsor can write a post and ask you to post it on your blog for your readers.
- Sponsors can also ask you to write a sponsored post following a strict guideline.

Sponsored posts can come in any form. Therefore, you should be ready for anything. The good thing about sponsored posts is that your client has already given you an idea. Your job is to produce content, which can be easy—making sponsored posts near-easy money.

Furthermore, the more clients you work with, the easier it will be to get other bigger or better clients that pay way better. In other words, it will be much easier to sell yourself and at a higher rate.

### What you need to get started with sponsored posts

To start monetizing your blog through sponsored posts, you need to arm yourself with several things—a sponsored post checklist.

Sponsors look for things like:

- **You must have a healthy number of readers**: No sponsor will want to associate with a blogger that doesn't have an audience. How will they get new customers to form a blog that no one visits? Thus, ensure you have healthy traffic before reaching out to sponsors. That means you should have a growing number of readers every month, not just a stagnant number of audience, perhaps your family and friends that are doing you the favor of reading your blog after a constant reminder.

Thus, drive traffic to your blog—as discussed in the last chapter. Take advantage of social media, email marketing, SEO optimization, referrals, etc., to grow your blog reader base. The more targeted readers your blog has, the more attractive you shall be to sponsors.

- **Social media authority:** Even though all your posts will be on your blog, sponsors believe that if you have a robust social media following, you will help them get more readers and clients because, when you have a good social media following, you are likely to participate in conversations that will promote your blog and the sponsor's post in the process. You can also quickly get feedback from your posts that your sponsor can use to make their product/service better.
- **A good blog:** A well-organized blog performs very

well in SEO and a darling of readers. A clean and simple site has a very low bounce rate. People are likely to stay on the blog longer and click through to the sponsor's link for more information. Optimize your site, make it neat, fast, well-structured, and very simple to navigate. Write great content, use quality images—you can find royalty-free images on sites like Pixabay and Pexels—and don't forget to publish your terms and conditions for services, contact, Disclaimer, and privacy policy.

### Factors to consider before accepting to work with a sponsor

When choosing which sponsors to work with, consider:

### Fit

I know it is hard to see money come and go, but you cannot just work with any sponsor that approaches you. Vet all sponsors to ensure they are a good fit for your audience and brand.

#### What does a good-fit sponsor look like?

A good-fit sponsor is someone you can work with well and easily. It's a client with whom you can have a good symbiotic relationship. You will help the sponsor grow their brand and improve their sales, and they will pay you handsomely and improve your reputation.

Finding a good-fit sponsor is vital because a good-fit sponsor is a long-term client. They will give you stability, money will keep coming in, and such a sponsor will help uphold your reputation as a blogger.

On the other hand, a bad-fit sponsor may damage your reputation, costing you many good future clients. Remember that blogging is a business where your reputation matters a lot.

Also, it will be much easier to work with a sponsor whose work you understand. For example, if your niche is finance, it will be challenging to write for a brand specialized in pets and veterinary matters.

The content you write for your sponsor should also resonate with your audience. Don't make the content look more like an ad or as if you are copywriting. Your audience should come out of your blog feeling like they have learned something valuable that may help them in the future.

Even when you are writing a sponsored post for a client, ensure that your audience also gets valuable content.

The sponsor's website you are linking to should be on good terms with Google guidelines

When writing a sponsored post, you will have to link to the sponsor's website. Google takes links seriously. They use it as one of the major ranking factors. If you link to a poor-quality website, it will reflect badly on you and may even get you penalized. If you link to a good quality website adhering to all Google ranking guidelines, it will improve your ranking.

However, if you are uncertain of your sponsor's website, you should add a "no follow" tag to the link. A "no follow" tag will stop Google from holding you responsible for your sponsor's link and won't use these links in ranking. You can do this by going to your blog dashboard.

If you are using WordPress, click on Code Editor or Text Editor. Find the hyperlink of the website you have linked to and add rel="nofollow."

For example if the website you are linking to has this hyper-link <ahref=https://sponsorwebsite.com"> Sponsor's Blog</a> change it to <ahref="rel="nofollow">Sponsor's Blog</a>.

You can learn more about "no follow" tags from WPbeginner

https://www.wpbeginner.com/beginners-guide/how-to-add-nofollow-links-in-wordpress/

Ensure you inform your sponsor that you added "no follow" tags to their links because the sponsor may be counting on these links to improve their domain authority.

### Getting Started With Sponsored Posts

At this point, you should have a traffic-ready blog and can start prospecting for sponsor clients. Sponsors may find you on their own, or you may have to reach out to them. Either way, you should be ready for both.

Here are the steps you should take to get started with sponsored posts:

### Step 1: Create a profile for sponsored opportunities

As mentioned earlier, some clients will find you on their own. When they do, they should find a profile that will make them hire you. Even clients that you reach out to will look at your profile before they consider working with you.

It's in your best interest to make your profile welcoming, exciting, and as detailed as you can without being overly wordy. Here, the old saying, quality over quantity, applies. Make your profile short but highly effective.

For example, don't say, "My blog is about fitness and health." Instead, say, "My blog is about people who are looking to get inspired, motivated, and guided towards living a healthy lifestyle, keeping fit, being happy and proud of themselves, and looking gorgeous without selling their souls." When someone reads the former statement, working with you will excite them.

### Step 2: Collect information about your site

Clients, especially sponsored clients, obsess over numbers. Before they hire you or consider hiring you, they must check to see the kind of numbers you got. These include:

- **Your site's statistics:** How many visitors do you get in a typical month, week, or during the day? What is your bounce rate? What is your click-through rate— How many times do people click on your site when you appear on search engines? What is your domain authority? What is your search engine traffic? You can find all this information on Google Analytics or any other tool you use to analyze your blog's performance.
- **Your social media statistics:** How many followers do you have on your chosen social media channels, i.e., Twitter, Instagram, Facebook, Snapchat, LinkedIn, and others? How many people have engaged with you through comments, shares, and likes in the past month?
- **Your email list:** How many people do you have on

your email list? How many subscribers do you add to your list per month? Out of all these people, how many of them actively engage with you?

## Step 3: Decide on your fees

This step is crucial because you must charge a good fee for writing for sponsors. Some bloggers make $750 to $1,000 per post. However, that will only happen after you've been in the game for a while and garnered a good following.

When starting, don't charge anything less than $250 per post. It takes a lot of time and effort to write a post that will benefit your readers and promote the sponsor's brand. You are giving your sponsors more customers to improve their bottom line; you deserve the remuneration for it.

If you are lucky to land a bigger brand, you will need to charge more. They are hard to work with sometimes.

Some people use Social Blue Book to help calculate their value based on their stats and blog outreach. My advice is to pitch double the value Social Blue Book gives you. You can then bargain at that double value. I advocate for this because many bloggers say that Social Media Book is conservative with its valuation.

## Step 4: Join blogger networks for sponsored posts

Many networks provide a platform for bloggers to find sponsors. These are good places to learn while earning before you start pitching to headhunted clients.

Such platforms include:

- Valued Voice https://www.valuedvoice.com/
- Aspire IQ https://app.aspireiq.com/creators/signup
- Massive Sway https://www.massivesway.com/
- Seeding Up www.seedingup.com
- BlogHer https://apply.shemedia.com/#aboutyou

**Step 5: Start reaching out to brands**

If you know of a brand in your niche that produces a product you would like to share with and promote to your audience, reach out to them via email—email outreach.

A simple email message can make all the difference. Here's a template you can customize accordingly:

*"Hello there:*

*I am emailing you in regards to your product. I wanted to know whether you work with bloggers to promote your products?*

*I have been using [product X[ for a year now, and I have to say, it produces great results. I would love to feature it in my blog, along with the results and benefits I have observed. By doing this, I hope to turn my readers into your loyal customers.*

*My blog gets x traffic per month, and I have x social media following. I believe partnering with you will be beneficial to us both.*

*Thank you for your time, and I am looking forward to hearing from you."*

**Step 6: Save brand emails and contacts**

After a sponsor accepts to work with you and you work well, save their email and contact details. After some time, like a month or a couple of weeks, you can ask them if they want to partner with you again.

Recontacting your contacts will help you get more opportunities in the future from a brand that you have a good previous working experience, thereby increasing your chances of success.

### Step 7: Keep updating your stats and optimizing your site

Many bloggers forget to update their stats and optimize their blogs consistently. These two factors are your central selling point. As your numbers grow, so will your charges. And brands are very keen on your numbers. They want to make sure that they will be getting good customers from you.

So, keep optimizing your blog, work on producing other great attractive content, keeping looking for a new audience, and when you get them, update your stats.

### Action step

Sponsored posts alone can help you make good money from blogging. Some people choose to focus on this alone. But first, you have to make sure that you are a well-established blogger.

Once you create a blog with a good following, healthy traffic, and valuable information, start pitching to clients.

## Dropshipping: Making Money Blogging through Dropshipping

As a blogger, you have an asset that everyone is looking for: an engaged audience, including your regular traffic and your followers on social media—you are rich in customers. You can—and should—take advantage of your opportunity to sell to them.

You don't have to produce products, have inventory, worry about shipping, or anything else to make money from your blog. You can do that, yes, but you don't have to. All you have to do is avail products on your blog.

For example, if your niche is women fashion, find an online supplier that makes gorgeous women fashion products and make a deal with the supplier to sell their products on your blog.

When someone buys a product from you, you send the customer's details to the supplier, along with the agreed-upon sale price. The supplier will then fulfill the order and ship it to the client. You are just an intermediary. Your job is just to post and promote products within your niche. Besides, you get to pick your prizes for those products.

A blogger called Sarah makes over $4 million a year from Dropshipping on her blog. Check her out on her blog Million Dollar Shop.

At the lowest level, Dropshipping will require you to create a store on your blog. From there, you will attract and motivate your audience to buy items from you. The trick is to ensure that these products relate to your niche and that they solve your audiences' pain points or struggles. When that's the case, it will be much easier for them to buy products from you.

## How to Get Started With Dropshipping

Get started on drop-shipping by implementing the following steps:

### Step 1: Optimize your blog

Before you start implementing any blog monetization approach, make sure your blog is successful.

Optimize your blog to give the best user experience and rank well on search engines. Write captivating content, get a solid following, and take advantage of social media and email marketing. Ensure that most of your customers are active; that they communicate, subscribe, and engage with you in various ways and means. Doing this will make converting your audience into paying customers easier.

### Step 2: Conduct market research

Before you decide which product to dropship, conduct intensive market research to find popular products that can resonate with your audience.

Your market research will involve cultivating in-depth knowledge of your regular audience and prospects—what they would want—and knowledge on products that will resonate well with them.

### How to do a market research

To conduct market research:

### Capitalize on trends

Recognize trending products in your niche earlier. Keep an eye out for products newly trending in your niche. Keep in mind that there're real trends and fads.

Fads are products that trend for a short while because of novelty (unfamiliarity) or a gimmick. They usually die out quickly when the steam is over.

Make Money Online Blogging

On the other hand, trends are new products on the market that genuinely satisfy a need or solve peoples' problems. Something that people will keep using for a long time.

The best ways to keep a lookout for these products include:

Social listening – Look for trending hashtags on social media. Which products within your niche are trending right now?

- **Google Trends:** As we observed before, Google Trends can tell you which products are trending, with a forecast of how a product will perform over time.
- **Trend Hunter:** The Trend Hunter site focuses on helping you find trending products, topics, and other relevant data you can use. It is a "trend community" that uses real humans and artificial intelligence to get new insights and opportunities. Make the best out of this platform.
- **Reddit:** Reddit is a social forum that people interact, communicate, and answer each other questions. It also showcases different trending topics in any niche. This forum serves as a hotspot for finding new trending ideas and topics.

### Read customer reviews on already existing products

Listening to what people are saying is probably the best way to learn about the best products to sell or dropship. All you have to do is go to other online stores like amazon.com and read reviews on popular products.

Amazon has a section for bestselling products, most wished For products, and Amazon movers and shakers. Etsy.com has

Etsy's most wanted, Etsy Bestselling items and Etsy's most popular items. eBay has Trending on eBay.

Visit these pages to see products in your niche performing well and what people are saying about them. The fact is, if a product is already selling well, chances are, it will continue to sell over time.

## Use keywords

Search engines are also good sources of information on trending products. This strategy will work best even for your blog because you will be selling products that are already performing well on the search engines that many people are searching for and want. Use the keyword research tools we discussed earlier to research products searched for multiple times.

Besides the keyword tools we discussed, here are others you can use for product research:

- EtsyRank
- Alibaba Hot Keywords

## Research profit margins

You should sell products that will allow you to make good profits. It takes a lot of time to make a blog, market it, find an audience, and sell products. Ensure that what you make will account for your work and the costs involved in creating a valuable asset. Expensive-to-produce products will have a lower profit margin than products that don't take much to produce. Also, consider how much it will cost you to ship, hold, and promote your items.

Small, lightweight products are the cheapest to ship. Products that people consume faster will move faster than long-lasting products. Consider these and other such factors when doing your research.

### Check-in your competition

As you can imagine, if your competition is struggling, chances are, people are not responding well to that product. If they are thriving, you can thrive too. The trick is to have one advantage over the competition and play to it heavily.

Analyze your competitor's success to identify some tricks you can use to one-up them. Analyze their failures with the same energy to figure out mistakes you should avoid and get an edge over them.

### Step 3: Look for reliable manufactures and distributors

Success at dropshipping comes down to customer satisfaction. If your supplier packs ineffective products, doesn't get the customer details right, and delivers products late, you will get a bad reputation that can kill your business. Some suppliers can even reach a point where they fail to have the inventory you would like for your business.

A reliable supplier:

- **Ensures that you stay updated on their inventory:** Such suppliers will give you real-time stock information and what you can work with readily, which will help you set up your online store.
- **Delivers high-quality products:** Products' quality determines your success. Therefore, they must be 100% effective, and you should be 100% confident that your audience will get what they pay for and want.
- **Has in place good return and refund policies:** There're always be unhappy customers who would

want to return some of the products they have bought. Sometimes, they may have gotten a measurement wrong while placing an order, and they would like to return or exchange the item. The supplier you work with must accept returns to make you look good to your customers.

- **Must also organize for shipping:** The essence of a Dropshipping business is to have the supplier in charge of distribution. Make sure that they deliver on time and have a reliable tracking process.

Here are some reliable suppliers you can work with:

- Shopify: https://www.shopify.com/dropshipping
- Oberlo: https://www.oberlo.com/dropshipping
- Alibaba/Aliexpress:https://m.alibaba.com/dropship-suppliers.html
- Spocket: https://www.spocket.co/
- SaleHoo: https://www.salehoo.com/
- Doba (https://www.doba.com/
- Wholesale 2B: https://www.wholesale2b.com/
- National Dropshippers: https://www.nationaldropshippers.com/

### Step 4: Test the market

It is always wise to start small to see how your audience responds to a product before you go big. If people love what you sell, you can then expand your online store. If they don't, try something else or promote your products better.

### Step 5: Promote! Promote! Promote!

Promote on all your social media platforms, your blog, and paid ads. Work with influencers and any other person that will help your business grow. That is the sure way to get more customers and a blog audience.

Affiliate marketing is the other way to monetize a blog:

### Affiliate Marketing: Making Money Through Affiliate Marketing—A Must-Do For All Bloggers

Affiliate marketing is the most popular monetization technique used by most bloggers. It is the simplest and most effective way of generating a passive income from your blog over the long term. If done right, you can make over $50,000 a month passively.

Affiliate marketing is the process of referring your audience to a company's or brand's website or products and earning a commission for every purchase your audience makes through your affiliate link.

### How it works

When you sign up for an affiliate program like Amazon, the platform will allow you to access products you can include in your blog—and their affiliate links.

When blogging and you happen to mention these products, copy and paste these links highlighting that particular product. When readers click on your links, it will redirect them to the merchant's website. If they make a purchase, you receive a percentage commission of what they pay.

It is that simple, and you will continue making money for as long as your blog is up and running.

One key thing to note is that affiliate marketing should not be your only income source unless you are well established and have many active followers. That's because it's largely a passive way of making money from a blog.

Affiliate marketing won't get you rich quickly. You will require some patience to build trust, get an actively clicking audience, and the commissions are a fraction of the selling price of the product you are selling.

Nonetheless, affiliate marketing is a must-do for all bloggers. Here are the reasons why you should consider it.

### It gives your audience more value

When blogging, you may come upon a product you know will help your audience. Instead of telling them to look for the product, you can provide a link that can quickly take them to that product, making their job much easier. Your audience will benefit from your affiliation as much as you do.

Furthermore, when you get discounts for your affiliation with a specific brand or product, you will pass on that discount to your audience, giving them more value by ensuring that they pay a much lower price than the original market price.

Your audience will be delighted with you, which will turn them into loyal followers.

### When you have a strong connection with a product

If you are passionate about a product that you keep mentioning in your articles, affiliate marketing will ensure that you'll get paid for it.

If you love a product and believe that it will add value to your audience, you will blog about it or write a review. In the process, you can include an affiliate link that will take your audience to the product.

If you have other products you have talked about but didn't include affiliate links, look for affiliate links for them. It's a win-win for everyone.

### If you have a good connection with your audience

If you have a good, trusting, and respectful relationship with your audience, it will be easier for them to trust what you recommend, even more than they would trust other marketers and influencers. That's because your audience knows that you have their best interest at heart, and there's no chance you will recommend a defective or poor quality product.

Ensure that whatever you recommend is the best product that will be very useful for your audience. Your reputation depends on it.

Let's discuss how to get started with affiliate marketing:

### How to Get Started With Affiliate Marketing

Here's how to implement affiliate marketing and make money from it:

### Step 1: Optimize your blog

Like all the other monetization techniques, your blog should be performing well. I am talking about increasing healthy traffic, good ranking, following all the Google guidelines, good engagement with your audience, and a great social media following.

## Step 2: Get to know your audience

To be good at affiliate marketing, you have to know what your audience wants. Successful affiliate marketers know [exactly] what their audience wants and how to sell it to them. You should write your content in a manner that motivates your audience to purchase because you only earn when they buy from your affiliate links.

Research your audience as much as possible. Read through their comments, communicate with them to realize their pain points, then recommend a product that will solve their problems or make their lives better.

It's also essential that you promote in-demand products needed by people that are actively looking for and buying them. When recommending products, give people a sense of urgency or great desire for the product because, as I've mentioned, you only get your affiliate commission when people buy using your affiliate links.

## Step 3: Conduct research on the affiliate products you want to feature on your blog

You cannot sell or recommend something you don't know intimately. One rule of commerce is to know and love your product to sell it well. When you have intimate knowledge of the products you promote to your audience, you will have a great selling point, and you will naturally write content that will lure people into making purchases.

Where it's possible, try out some of your affiliate products before you recommend them. For one, you will know [exactly] what you are talking about, and secondly, you will add some personal touch to your blog posts. People love personal recommendations; they will easily trust you if they see that you are also using the product you recommend to them.

Be honest; don't just talk about the good points. You will come off as biased. Include some of the downsides, if there are any, to make you seem genuine and interested in your audiences' well-being.

### Step 4: Find affiliate programs to join

Find merchants that offer affiliate partnerships. You can either partner with a company or decide to work with a network. From personal experience, it's better to do both.

Partnering with a company means promoting that company's product. Working with a network entails promoting products of companies that the network represents. Both options require signing up and agreeing to the terms and conditions of the partnership.

Some of the common rules of affiliate programs partnership include—or at least, these are the rules that amazon.com insists on:

- Don't mention the prizes of products on your blog because prizes change with time.
- Mention in your blog that you might earn a commission for the products you have recommended.
- Your review or comments should be on pure evidentiary facts. Don't mislead people.
- Amazon.com insists that you shouldn't shorten any of the affiliate links they provide.

Here is how you can sign up for the Amazon.com affiliate program:

Go to their Affiliate Homepage and click on "Sign Up."

You can either create a new account or sign up using your regular amazon account—the account you use for everyday purchases.

The platform will ask you for personal details like your name, email address, residency, etc. Additionally, you will also have to provide a link to your blog, the one you will be using for your affiliate links. You can even include a link to your app, YouTube channel, and any other websites you may have. The limit is 50.

The next step is choosing an ID for your blog; Amazon will use this to identify you. For example, you can use qtrz908. Next, choose the categories of products within your niche.

The next page will be more about your blog. The Amazon Affiliate program will ask about how you intend to attract buyers to your blog, your link-building techniques, your average monthly visitors, and why you want to join an affiliate program.

Once you complete that straightforward process, you will enter a verification page. Type in your phone number and click on "Call Me Now." Amazon will call you with a PIN. Enter this pin in the box provided. Finish up by entering your payment method, that is, where you would like to receive your commissions. At this point, your application is complete.

After entering your newly created account, you will see two options, i.e., Quick Links and Browse for products. Use the Quick Links options to find a link to a particular product you want to promote. Use the Browse for products option when you want to browse through categories to find a product you want to promote.

When you find your product, click on "Get Link" to receive your affiliate link.

You can further customize the link provided, the images, color, texts, and other features. Once satisfied with what you have, copy the link and paste it on your blog.

Besides the Amazon Affiliate program—often called Amazon Associates—here are the other affiliate networks you can join:

- ShareASale: click on "monetize your content" and sign up for an affiliate account. This network has over 3,900 affiliate programs in 40 different categories.
- ClickBank: As one of the most extensive affiliate networks, Clickbank has clients worldwide and has paid commissions of over $4.2 billion.
- CJ Affiliate: This is another big affiliate platform with more than 3000 merchants.
- Flex Offers: This program has over 12,000 merchants.
- Pepperjam: This program has over 1500 merchants.
- Rakuten Marketing: This affiliate program has 1000 merchants.

- eBay partner network: The eBay partner network is one of the oldest, most trusted affiliate networks.

To find companies providing affiliate programs, use the following search parameters (preferably on Google)

"Your niche" + Affiliate program. For example, "women jewelry affiliate program."

"Niche product" + affiliate program. For example, "khaki pants affiliate products."

"A keyword" + affiliate. For example, "Italian cuisine affiliate."

"A keyword" + Affiliate program. For example, "Italian cuisine affiliate program."

"A keyword" + Affiliate product. For example, "boots affiliate product."

"Product name" + affiliate. For example, "timberlands affiliate."

Agree to the terms of the companies you will find online. Make sure that they are legit and offer valuable products.

To conclude:

Affiliate marketing should be a must-do for every blogger. It will keep money coming in for the longest time possible and is one of the best ways to generate a passive income from blogging.

## EBooks: Making Money From eBooks

If you have a passion for writing eBooks, why not write them and sell them on your blog?

EBook distributors like Amazon.com take 30% of your sales profit. 30% is a lot of money, and that's without factoring in the taxes you have to pay and other expenses like an editor, book formatter, and book cover designer.

It's much cheaper and convenient to sell your eBooks on your blog. For one, you don't pay any additional costs, and secondly, you easily avail your eBook to your readers.

If you want to monetize your blog audience through ebook publication, here's what you need to do:

### Getting Started With eBooks

To start monetizing your blog using an eBook:

### Step 1: Find a good eBook idea to write about

The first step to writing a good eBook is finding a great idea within your niche, an idea that has the potential to generate sales.

An eBook that has the potential to generate sales must be beneficial and useful to your readers. It should resonate well with their interests and needs and solve some of their core problems. It should also interest or excite you; you should personally love your eBook because it would be nearly impossible to write the book without passion.

Therefore, do some research to find a topic that has a real, evidentiary demand on the market.

Here is how you can get started with your search for a great idea:

## Begin by thinking about that one subject that interests you the most

Think of a topic that you would happily explore and write about, even if there was no money involved. It could be a previous blog topic that you might want to expound on or a topic you have become an expert in.

When writing your blogs, you may have to touch on other ideas to keep your blog going, or readers entertained. But there are times you will write on topics that you have a true passion for, your true expertise. You should write an eBook on such topics and monetize them.

## Think about topics that a great majority of your audience crave for

Write about something that truly interests you and that your audience will truly value. You should be confident that your target audience will love the topic you have decided to choose. c

You can discover what your audience genuinely loves by:

- **Asking them:** As novel as it sounds, asking your audience what they would love to read pays off. You can do this through your email list by sending an email newsletter asking about which topic idea will interest them as an eBook. Tally their response and find the most popular answer and use it as a topic. You can also use quizzes and surveys.
- **Look at your best-performing articles:** Analyze your blog to find articles that got the most engagement, traffic, comments, shares, and likes. Expound on that particular topic in an eBook.
- **Review your readers' conversations:** Find a

consistently asked question on your blog comments, email, and social media. Find themes that keep recurring, then use them as an idea for your eBook.

## Research your competition

A word of advice:

Before venturing into any project, be it writing your blog articles, selling products, or finding ideas for your eBooks, always do a little research on your competition.

It is a good idea to know what other people in your niche are doing before you make a move. Even if you are coming with a different idea or style, take a look at how people responded before and how you can make them respond better with your style. The same applies to eBooks.

Visit amazon.com to see some books written on your idea. Look at the reviews and purchases. Go further and look at blogs in your niche that have written eBooks on your idea. Steer clear from topics that have thousands of eBooks and books. When starting, you should write on a topic with low to medium competition. You can then build up from there.

As was the case with keywords, I would advise starting with long-tail keywords before you start competing on the short-tail keywords because you get a chance to stand out and gain authority.

However, if your content is unique and significantly better than other eBooks in your industry, then write it and explain to your audience why they should go for your eBook and not your competitors.

**Do keyword research**

Keyword research will help you find what people are truly searching for and want. The keywords you find should be within your niche.

The same keywords tools we discussed earlier will work great here too, but you can also add TwinWord to your list of keywords research tools. It works great for finding topic ideas.

**Step 2: Develop an outline and structure for your eBook**

Once you find a good topic you can write about, it is time to start the actual work: writing the book. The first thing you need to do is to have an outline and structure for your book.

Here is how you can go about it.

**Start with the outline**

Your outline is your foundation for writing; use it everywhere, including when writing your blog posts. A fundamental outline follows the following rules:

It should have a good title that will captivate your readers' interest: You should make sure that your title will make people want to buy your book.

Therefore:

- Don't make it too generic. Instead, choose a tile that will stand out among all your competitors.
- Make the title exciting. Exciting titles have elements like emotional appeal, humor, a play of words, words that invoke curiosity or quickly grab readers attention.
- The title should be easy to remember. Your readers

may see your eBook on your blog while browsing through your content. They may not buy it then, but if the name is easy to remember, they can search for it days later when they want to learn more and perhaps buy it.

- Include keywords to optimize for search engine searches.

You don't have to come up with a captivating title right away. You can write your entire book with a working title and then come back later to think of a title

- Jot down the key takeaways from your eBook.
- Write the key questions that your readers usually ask, and make sure you answer all of them in the content.
- Arrange the main themes into chapters.

Your chapters need to be cohesive. In other words, your eBook should have a flow from the beginning to the end.

### Do intensive research and include links to relevant studies and additional sources in your eBook

People love content corroborated with facts and research they can confirm. It makes them believe your content. Take advantage of these and include some relevant researches made on your topic.

### Start writing

Begin with a killer introduction. If your readers get bored with your introduction or eBook description, there is no chance that they will buy or continue reading your content. While the content, chapters, and studies matter, your introduction matters more because it sets the book's tone.

Conclude your book with a call to action. When readers finish reading your eBook, they should feel inspired to take action on what they have learned. Ensure you write in a way that inspires and motivates them to take the Call-to-Action. You can do this in the summary section where you:

- Recap the big ideas.
- Remind them of the key takeaways.
- Have clear instructions and action steps.

A well-researched outline will give you a clear idea of what to write, which will make writing your eBook easier.

### Step 3: Pick a file format for your eBook

There are five main file formats to use with eBooks. The format you decide to use will depend on its contents.

For example, if you have included tons of images and a design change design will make the eBook look bad or unwelcoming, you may need to use a format that ensures a fixed layout.

Here are some of the formats you should consider:

### Portable Document Format (PDF) eBook File Format

PDF is the most popular file format we have today because it's the easiest to publish, download and read. Besides, you can easily save your Microsoft Word document or Google Doc as a PDF.

The disadvantage of the PDF file format is that it lacks a feature called "reflowable." Reflowability is when you can access your file on multiple devices. You must physically transfer it to another device or upload it in a cloud (like

Google Drive), where, if you want to read it with another device, you will have to download it again.

Moreover, the PDF file format is easy to share for free, and if one of your audience distributes it, people will not come back to buy from you again.

### EPUB File Format

Many eBook publishers prefer this format because it's viewable on multiple devices, including computers, tablets, smartphones, and eReaders. Another benefit is that this format is reflowable and has a fixed layout. Therefore, if your eBook has tons of images and a specific, unique design, the design will adapt to different devices.

The only disadvantage of this format is that Amazon Kindle doesn't support it.

### Kindle File Format (KFF, AZW and AZW3)

If you would like to sell your eBook through Amazon, this file format will be ideal for you. These file formats only work with Kindle or other Amazon-owned apps.

### TXT File Format

If you would like to publish your eBook in plain text that is exceptionally long, you should use this format. This format is easily downloadable. However, you will rarely find people publishing eBooks in TXT format.

I would recommend using the EPUB file format for your eBooks.

### Step 4: Design your eBook

From the book cover to the content, your eBook design should grab your readers' attention and keep them interested in the eBook.

Your eBook should match the aesthetics of your blog. It should be neat, captivating, and professional.

The image or graphics you use on your cover should be original. Please don't copy and paste someone else's works; it sends a bad picture to your readers. If you don't know how to make original graphics, you can look for a graphic designer on websites like 99Designs.

Here are some tools you can use to design your eBook

- Designrr: https://designrr.io/
- Canva: https://www.canva.com/
- Visme: https://partner.visme.co/v2/login
- LucidPress: https://lucidpress.com/pages/
- Venngage: https://venngage.com/

### Step 5: Sell and promote

Build a specific landing page on your site for your eBook. In your landing page, include a good, compelling description of your eBook—talk about why your audience needs the book and how it will be useful for them.

Find a way to make them want the book; the marketing strategies you used for Dropshipping can come in handy here: create a sense of urgency, build curiosity, present your book as the key to solving one of your audiences' problems, and making their lives better.

Ensure you explain the process of purchasing and downloading the eBook, then Promote! Promote! Promote!

Use your email list to send newsletters concerning your eBook. Use your social media pages, influencers, employ ads —both Google and social media ads— and promote your book through your blog articles and any other method you know will work out.

The better you are at promoting your eBook, the better your chances of income generation.

Another effective way of monetizing your blog is through online courses.

**Online Courses: Monetizing Your Blog Through Digital Course**

Online courses are a multi-billion dollar e-learning market with an annual growth rate of 14.6%. Projections show that the e-learning market will be worth $374.3 billion by 2026.

People became more welcoming to online courses during the COVID-19 pandemic. It has become more convenient to learn online than to attend lectures or classes physically. Besides, people have become increasingly hungry for self-attained expertise and improvement.

We all want to stand out and make it in this highly competitive world. Therefore, your lessons or courses are timeless and limitless. People will still view and learn from a course on your website ten years from now because facts don't change.

Jump on the online courses train today; it has tremendous benefits, including:

- A chance to increase your income: Digital courses are an effective way to earn a passive income.
- It can help you scale up your business. You can teach people about your products/services.
- More freedom. Remember, you don't have to be personally present to teach. All you have to do is create a video course, post it on your blog, market it, and people will subscribe to watch it at will.
- It gives you more authority in your niche. You can use this authority in other fields like sponsored posts, affiliate marketing, and Dropshipping.

### Getting Started With Online Courses

Here are the steps to monetizing your blog using online courses:

### Step 1: Ensure your courses are relevant to your audience

The first and most vital factor to pay attention to when monetizing your blog through online courses is to ensure that the course is within your niche, relevant to your blog theme, and of high value to your audience.

Don't teach just about anything. Find something that will resonate with your audience because the more niche you are, the easier and quicker it will be to make money from your digital course.

### Step 2: Find content for your courses

This step is easy.

Start by analyzing your best-performing articles; ten should do. Use them to get an idea of what course to create. You can even turn your articles into video tutorials.

Furthermore, you can answer your readers' most popular questions to get ideas for your videos. Ideas for your content are everywhere. Once you get started and get the momentum going, everything else will fall into place.

### Step 3: Add a course tab on your blog

Once things start moving, you should make it very easy for your readers to find your courses.

One of the best ways to do this is by adding a "course" tab on your blog homepage. When they click on this tab, it should redirect them to your courses.

The following YouTube video will show you how to add a "course tab" on your blog:

https://youtu.be/4Sff2BcHXvo

### Step 4: Add an "enroll now" or "buy now" button to your blogs

When people are browsing through your blog or reading your posts, it means they have a genuine interest in your content. Therefore, give them a quick direction to your other informative content, your courses.

You should add hyperlinks at appropriate points in your posts or include a quick banner at the end of every post that advertises your online courses. You can even go further to add a blog pop-up advertising your course.

Encourage people to take action on your hyperlinks using the "Enroll Now" and "buy now" buttons. The more you sell, the more willing buyers you will get.

### Step 5: Grow your audience

Did you know that you can borrow an audience from other blogs? It is simple.

Ask a successful blogger with a large audience if you can write guest posts for them and when you get the green light, ensure you include a backlink that takes readers back to your blog or directly to your courses. Blog posting will help you get good traffic from someone else's audience.

### Step 6: Turn your courses into other income opportunities

Once your online courses start picking up, find ways to capitalize them and use them to create more income-generating opportunities. For example, you can do this by creating a group or a forum for your audience, someplace where they can discuss with each other what they have learned from you.

Doing this will encourage engagement and give you more ideas you can use to generate more revenue.

### Action step

You can monetize your blog from the first day—first post—and you should. However, remember that, in essence, monetizing a blog boils down to monetizing your audience. Therefore, the larger your audience, the higher your income-generating chances.

That's why my advice to you is simple:

Even as you monetize from the go, focus on growing your audience by offering them the best value possible. The more value you provide, the more income you stand to generate from your blog.

# BONUS: A 34-DAY PLAN FOR STARTING A MONEY-MAKING BLOG

This bonus chapter takes everything you've learned from this guidebook and turns it into a 34-day action plan you can use to create an income-generating blog.

Let's dive into it:

### Action Plan 1: Understand blogging basics

- **Day 1, activity 1:** Learn about blogging, its importance (why you need to start a blog), how it differs from a website, and the history of how blogging started and became what it is today.
- You can also read through a couple of blogs to get a feel of how it works.

### Action Plan 2: Choose a Niche

Once you master the basics, focus on starting your blog. This process begins with choosing a niche.

- **Day 2, activity 2:** Brainstorm and make a list of all niches you are comfortable working with—take your time with this.
- **Day 3, activity 3:** Sieve through the list to find 5-6 different niches you feel you can comfortably enter and ensure to explain why these are your best niches.
- **Day 4, activity 4:** Out of the 5-6 niches, find three that have the potential of making money on the current market.

**Action Plan 3: Choose A Blogging Platform That Fits Your Needs**

Next, find the best platform that you can use well.

- **Day 5, activity 5:** We discussed over eight blogging platforms. Analyze each thoroughly, ensuring to consider both the benefits and disadvantages of each, budget, search engine friendliness, ease of use, etc.
- **Day 6: Activity 6:** Consider which platform offers more money-making opportunities.
- **Day 7, activity 7:** Conduct extra research to find blogging platforms you can customize to suit your desired theme and best user experience.

**Action Plan 4: Set Up Your Blogging Platform Of Choice**

NOTE: I would personally recommend working with wordpress.org or Ghost.

- **Day 8, activity 8:** On day 8, set up your blogging platform. This process starts with purchasing a custom domain based on your chosen niche and a hosting package.

- **Day 9, activity 9:** Consider the plugins and themes offered by your platform of choice to see which would be perfect for your audience.
- **Day 10, activity 10:** Customize your blog. Try many different styles before you settle on the one you will stick with for the long haul.

**Action Plan 5: Drive Traffic To Your Blog Through Social Media**

Find people to visit and subscribe to your blog. Start with all your social media accounts.

- **Day 11, activity 11:** Announce your blog on all your social media platforms, making sure to include your blog address in the profile—the bio section.
- **Day 12, activity 12:** Be very active on social media; engage and interact with your audience through comments, keep sharing content from your blog, add visuals, create groups and forums for your blog, etc.
- **Day 13, activity 13:** Find influencers on social media that can promote your blog. You can also use paid advertising.

**Action Plan 6: Drive Traffic To Your Blog Through Email Marketing**

- **Day 14, activity 14:** Start building your email list.
- **Day 15, activity 15:** Focus on learning how to write captivating and compelling emails that will lead to the necessary conversions.
- **Day 16, activity 16:** Start sending audience nurturing emails to your email list.

**Action Plan 7: Drive Traffic To Your Blog Through SEO**

Organic traffic is the secret to creating a blog that generates a passive income.

- **Day 17, activity 17:** Read Google guidelines on setting up and optimizing your blog/website for search engines.
- **Day 18, activity 18:** Apply all the Google suggestions on your blog.
- **Day 19, activity 19:** Focus on leveraging keywords and the other SEO tips we discussed earlier in this guidebook.

**Action Plan 8: Monetize Your Blog Through Partnerships Aka Sponsored Posts**

As mentioned, sponsored posts are one of the easiest ways to monetize your blog audience.

- **Day 20, activity 20:** Optimize your blog for brands and create a great profile that is attractive to sponsored opportunities.
- **Day 21, activity 21:** Analyze your blog, collect and present relevant information for your clients. The information you gather should include the number of traffic you receive per month, the number of social media followers, your email list, and any other pertinent data.
- **Day 22, activity 22:** Start reaching out to brands and join blogger networks for sponsored posts.

### Action plan 9: Monetize Your Blog Through Dropshipping

- **Day 23, activity 23:** Conduct extensive market research to find profitable products you can drop ship to your audience.
- **Day 24, activity 24:** Find reliable suppliers, drop shippers, and distributors for the products you have decided to promote to your audience.
- **Day 25, activity 25:** Create an online store on your blog and test the market to see how people respond to your drop shipped product before you go all in.

### Action Plan 10: Monetize Your Blog Through Affiliate Marketing

- **Day 26, activity 26:** Study your audience to know [exactly] what they want and how best to sell it to them.
- **Day 27, activity 27:** Conduct in-depth research to find affiliate products you can feature and promote on your blog; as mentioned, these products should provide your audience with value.
- **Day 28, activity 28:** Find affiliate programs to join or companies you can work with that have an affiliate program.

### Action plan 11: Monetize Your Blog With eBooks

- **Day 29, activity 29:** Find a good eBook idea to flesh out into a book. Here, it's best to play to topics you are passionate about and topics that your audience wants to learn more about, then outline the book.

- **Day 30, activity 30:** Think about which marketing strategies you shall use—and why you've chosen those approaches.
- **Day 31, activity 31:** Start writing!

**Action Plan 12: Monetize Your Blog Through Digital Course**

- **Day 32, activity 32:** Find course subjects relevant to your audience.
- **Day 33, activity 33:** Find content for your courses.
- **Day 34, activity 34:** Start selling the courses to your audience. Promote your courses to get a larger audience, create a course tab on your blog, and take advantage of social media and email marketing to get more audience.

Implementing these 34-steps will help ensure that you set yourself up for blogging success.

We have discussed these steps at length in this book. All you have to do is refer to the related sections to learn how to implement each of these steps. When you do, you will make money online from blogging.

# AFTERWORD

I wrote this guide hoping that it could help someone, perhaps you, create a successful, monetizable blog that generates an income month after month.

I have given you all the information you need to get started. The ball is now in your court. Remember that to score, you have to kick the ball, so start taking action today and implementing what you have learned!

One crucial thing to remember is that making money from blogging starts with a high-quality blog.

By this, I mean your blog should be well organized, themed, easy to navigate, and in compliance with all Google guidelines. Adhering to Google guidelines will help you provide your audience with the best user experience. Your blog should be well optimized for SEO. Good SEO assures high ranking, which is the most reliable way of getting high traffic.

Other critical actions you should take include:

- Leveraging social media
- Paid ads
- Referral traffic
- Guest posts
- Influencers marketing
- Backlinking
- Email marketing, etc.

Remember to produce the best content you can produce. Good content sells itself, and many bloggers will refer their audience to you—backlinking—if your content is the best in your niche.

Once you get all of that right, monetizing your blog and generating a substantial income from it will be near-effortless.

**-Darren Lamar**

Made in the USA
Columbia, SC
30 May 2021